WE ARE
CHRISTIANS
BECAUSE...

WE ARE CHRISTIANS BECAUSE...

ROBERT E. WELLS

Deseret Book

Salt Lake City, Utah

Library of Congress Cataloging in Publication Data

Wells, Robert E.
    We are Christians because.

    Includes index.
    1. Church of Jesus Christ of Latter-day Saints—
Apologetic works. 2. Mormon Church—Apologetic works.
I. Title.
BX8635.5.W45   1985   238'.9332   84-28762
ISBN 0-87747-639-X

Contents

Preface

Many people have never made the connection between the nicknames "Mormon," "LDS," or "Latter-day Saints" and the full, proper, official name of the church: "The Church of Jesus Christ of Latter-day Saints." To members of the Church, it may come as a surprise to learn that there are many people in the world who do not know that the Mormons are Christians. In fact, there are organized and well-financed efforts to confuse the public through erroneous statements that the Church is a non-Christian sect whose members do not believe in Christ.

The purpose of this book is to give members of The Church of Jesus Christ of Latter-day Saints and to all our friends twenty familiar, easy-to-remember pillars of our faith. These chapters are intended to dispel any doubts that we are Christians.

This book is not designed to be a source of contention, but rather a summary of those practices and doctrines that identify us as followers and worshipers of the Savior of mankind. We have always asked for the privilege of worshiping Almighty God according to the dictates of our own conscience, and we have always allowed others the same privilege. All persons are at their best when they worship their God. We respect their right to believe all that is sacred to them, and we ask that they allow us the same courtesy.

And finally, this book is not an official publication of The Church of Jesus Christ of Latter-day Saints. The author, and he alone, is responsible for its contents. It has been written on my own initiative and not at the request of the Church or of anyone else. The material is based on notes from my own sermons given over a period of years on these subjects and represents my own opinion on doctrines and policies except where quotations are used. It is my hope and prayer that the contents will be of interest and of use to all who read it.

I am grateful to my wife, Helen, and to my daughter Elayne, who have helped with the preparation of the manuscript. I also express appreciation to my secretary, Elaine Freeman, for typing the manuscript.

We Are Christians Because . . .

We Believe in God, the Eternal Father, and in His Son, Jesus Christ

For more than a century and a half, members of The Church of Jesus Christ of Latter-day Saints have declared to the world, "We Believe in God, the Eternal Father, and in His Son, Jesus Christ, and in the Holy Ghost." (Article of Faith 1.)

As Christians, the Latter-day Saints embrace and accept and obey the Ten Commandments, including the first commandment, which states: "Thou shalt have no other gods before me." (Exodus 20:3.) We believe that not only should we not worship any false gods or substitute gods, but also that we should have a clear and true picture in our minds and an understanding of the God that we do worship. In fact, a true concept of God is necessary for eternal life and exaltation in the world to come, for Jesus taught: "This is life eternal, that they might know thee the only true God, and Jesus Christ, whom thou hast sent." (John 17:3.)

We have no other Gods before us! We believe, as the scriptures so clearly teach, that there is no intermediary between God the Father and His many children on earth save Jesus Christ, His Son. He is the only authorized intermediary or advocate. We pray only to the Father, not to the Son nor to anyone else, and when we do pray, it is always in the name of the Son, Jesus Christ.

It is vitally important to us, as Christians, to worship, honor, exalt, and obey the same God, the same Heavenly Father, as Christ prayed to and called His own Father. Our concept of Deity is identical to that held by the ancient Christians. They understood, just as we today understand, that the three members of the

1

Godhead are three separate and distinct personages. The early Christians did not mix the three members of the Godhead into a blurred mental image of three-in-one yet one-in-three; that image came into theology some three hundred years or so after Christ's crucifixion and resurrection. The apostles and disciples who knew Him personally and who left their record in the scriptures that are now part of the New Testament clearly delineated between each of these personages whom we worship.

When Christ was baptized, the record states that (1) He was in the water; (2) a voice from heaven was heard saying "This is my beloved Son, in whom I am well pleased"; and (3) the Spirit of God, or Holy Ghost, descended upon Him like a dove. (See Matthew 3:16-17.) After Jesus' resurrection, Stephen, the martyr, looked up into heaven and saw Him, the Son of God, "standing on the right hand of God." (Acts 7:56.) There is no confusion: Stephen saw two Gods, one to the right of the other. He saw both the Father and the Son.

The unity of the Godhead, as though they were one, is reflected in the great intercessory prayer Jesus offered to His Father in the Upper Room before departing for the Garden of Gethsemane, when He said, "Father, glorify thou me with thine own self with the glory which I had with thee before the world was." (John 17:5.) Jesus worshiped the Father and prayed fervently to Him, demonstrating the individuality of their persons. Later He prayed for His disciples, for the Twelve Apostles and other converts, that they all should be preserved in unity, saying, "That they all may be one; as thou, Father, art in me, and I in thee, that they also may be one in us: that the world may believe that thou hast sent me." (John 17:21.) Repeatedly He stated the phrase "that they may be one, even as we are one." It would not be reasonable to think that all of the apostles and disciples should be merged into one essence, as some believe, nor to think that Christ, who was praying, was the same person as the Father to whom He prayed.

The true meaning of the prayer was that Christ desired that all should be united in heart, spirit, and purpose. The scriptures do not imply any mystical substance, but rather emphasize that each of the three whom we recognize as Deity is of the same mind as the others. Each would see situations alike; each would respond alike; each would be guided by the same principles of unerring equity and justice. It seems logical also that Jesus the Son would look like His Father, for that is what He said: "He that hath seen me hath seen the Father." (John 14:9.)

Joseph Smith, the Prophet of the Restoration, saw the Father and the Son standing together side by side in a column of light that was brighter than the noonday sun. He stated that their brightness and glory were beyond description. To this youth who prayed in a grove in the spring of 1820, the Father spoke: "This is My Beloved Son. Hear Him!" (Joseph Smith–History 1:17.) Had the Prophet indicated that this vision should cause anyone to worship him, Joseph, because of what he had seen, we would know that he was a fraud. He did not do this. Rather, he recounted the vision so that others would worship the Father, in the name of the Son, and by the power of the Holy Ghost. Joseph took no credit unto himself. No Christian prophet ever does; a Christian prophet teaches and preaches Jesus Christ.

On April 3, 1836, in a newly dedicated temple at Kirtland, Ohio, the Prophet again saw the resurrected Savior in a vision. This time Joseph was accompanied by Oliver Cowdery. His account is one of the finest descriptions of the resurrected Savior in all the literature of the world. He said: "We saw the Lord standing upon the breastwork of the pulpit, before us; and under his feet was a paved work of pure gold, in color like amber. His eyes were as a flame of fire; the hair of his head was white like the pure snow; his countenance shone above the brightness of the sun; and his voice was as the sound of the rushing of great waters, even the voice of Jehovah, saying: I am the first and the last; I am he who liveth, I am he who was slain; I am your advocate with the Father." (D&C 110:2-4.)

We truly have no other gods before us. Even with such experiences as Joseph Smith had, we do not pray to Joseph nor do we worship him. We worship God, our Heavenly Father!

Recently I was traveling on an airplane in a South American country. My seat companion was a sophisticated international engineer who spoke many languages and who had traveled widely. In our conversation, we managed to get around to religion, and I found an opportunity to explain and tell him about the origin of our beliefs, the first vision of Joseph Smith, and the many teachings of Jesus Christ found in the Book of Mormon, which was translated by Joseph through the power of God.

When I had finished, my seat companion commented, "You Mormons have surely built a magnificent shrine at Joseph Smith's grave site."

In surprise, I exclaimed, "*What* shrine? *What* grave site?"

"Why, that tall building in Salt Lake City with the gold angel on top. Isn't that a mausoleum or shrine of some kind where you worship your prophet?"

In dismay, I recognized his misunderstanding—no telling where it came from. He had mistaken the Salt Lake Temple for the grave site of Joseph Smith.

"Please allow me to explain that we definitely *are* Christians," I told him. "We *do* worship God the Father, in the name of His Son, Jesus Christ, and we do *not* worship any prophet or saint, modern or ancient. We do not worship the Prophet Joseph Smith, though we love and honor him. But we never pray to him. In our doctrine, philosophy, and practice, Joseph Smith is not an intermediary of any kind, nor is any other prophet or saint. Christ alone is our advocate with the Father"—and I repeated for emphasis—"*not* Mary, *not* Joseph, *not* Peter or James or John, nor any of the ancient prophets like Adam, Moses, or Abraham. No modern prophet like Joseph Smith or Brigham Young is ever worshiped or prayed to."

I went on to explain that the temple in Salt Lake City was not built to honor Joseph Smith nor is he even buried there. To make my point that we do not worship our prophets, I said, "Please believe me when I say that we never make a pilgrimage to where the Prophet Joseph is buried. As a matter of fact, I do not even know *where* he is buried!"

At this point I should like to spell out in a concise manner some of the roles and some of the attributes of each member of Deity as understood by the early Christian church and as taught today by The Church of Jesus Christ of Latter-day Saints. Please remember that "we claim the privilege of worshiping Almighty God according to the dictates of our own conscience, and allow all men the same privilege, let them worship how, where, or what they may." Everyone else is entitled to his own beliefs, and we feel that we also should be entitled to our own. Here is a summary of some of those basic concepts:

God the Father

1. His name is Elohim.

2. He is a personal being with a resurrected and glorified body.

3. He is the Father of our spirits. We lived with Him as His children. We are in His image.

4. He is infinite, all-knowing, all-powerful, unlimited, the Creator and Doer of all.

5. His personality is loving, kind, benevolent, patient, just, and merciful. At the same time He is jealous when we worship false gods, and He is zealous toward the principles of truth and righteousness.

6. He wants His children to have the opportunity to be resurrected, glorified, and exalted, so He has offered us a plan whereby we can become His heirs, co-heirs with His Son, Jesus Christ. This plan of salvation is very specific and was known to the early Christians. It is the same plan today and is taught as Christian doctrine by The Church of Jesus Christ of Latter-day Saints.

7. He sent His firstborn Son, our elder brother, and His Only Begotten Son in the flesh, to be our Savior, Redeemer, and Messiah.

Jesus Christ, the Son of God

1. His name is Jehovah in the Old Testament. He appeared to and talked with the ancient prophets. When He spoke, He did so on behalf of the Father, and He said what the Father would have said.

2. He is the first spirit child of our Heavenly Father, and thus our Elder Brother.

3. He was presented by our Heavenly Father in the council in heaven as our Savior and Redeemer in the Father's plan.

4. He was sent by the Father to be the Creator of this world and the Creator of worlds without number—all the stars, all the galaxies of space.

5. His earthly mother was the wonderful woman known as Mary, the wife of Joseph.

6. He paid the price for Adam's transgression; therefore, each of us will be resurrected.

7. He paid the price for our sins, if we will repent of them; therefore, if we accept His name and obey His commandments, we can become joint-heirs with Him in our Father's kingdom. He has redeemed or ransomed us, thus becoming our Redeemer.

8. He loved us enough to die for us so that we could, first, live again, and second, become exalted—the first automatically, the good with the bad, through his grace; but the second only upon condition of personal obedience and worthiness.

9. His earthly ministry is real, as recorded in the scriptures, with all the miracles, history, events, beauty, and tragedy. His resurrection also is a recorded fact.

10. He will personally judge us at the time of our death.

11. He will come again in glory and will reign upon the earth as the Lord of lords and King of kings.

12. He is the only one through whom salvation comes.

The Holy Ghost

1. He is called the Comforter and the Holy Spirit.

2. He does not have a body of flesh and bones, but is a personage of spirit.

3. He communicates knowledge; He is a teacher.

4. He witnesses and testifies of the Father and the Son.

5. He declares to man the attributes of the Father and the Son through the spirit.

6. He is a revelator.

7. He gives comfort and consolation.

8. The gift of the Holy Ghost is given to the baptized Christian by the laying on of hands.

9. Jesus directs the work of the Church through this third member of the Godhead.

10. He sanctifies.

In the modern world there are many false gods that many children of our Heavenly Father mistakenly worship. Some honor the gods of fame and fortune, placing things of the world foremost in their lives to the exclusion of the Father of our spirits and our Savior. Others, by their acts, would appear to worship a sport in a stadium, because on the Sabbath they choose to spend their time there instead of tending to their Christian duties on the "day of the Lord." Many are the ways in which we can offend and disappoint each and all three members of the Godhead.

As Christians, we strive to teach and preach the true and proper worship of our Heavenly Father. He lives. He loves us and hears and answers our prayers. His Son, our Lord Jesus Christ, also lives and is resurrected, glorified, and exalted. The Holy Ghost, the third member of the Godhead, is available to those who have faith in Jesus Christ, repent of their sins, enter the waters of baptism, and have hands laid upon their heads from a legal administrator of Jesus Christ.

In summary, we are Christians because we see Christ as the key to understanding and worshiping the Father. We teach of Christ, we preach of Christ, we prophesy of Christ, we worship Christ. He was with the Father and was the first of the Father's spirit children. Under the direction of the Father, He was the Creator of this earth and of worlds without number. He is Jehovah of the Old Testament, and He appeared to the ancient prophets. And in His earthly ministry, He calmed the wind and the waves, fed the multitude, walked on water, changed water to wine, healed the lepers, gave sight to the blind, made the crippled walk, raised the dead! As the resurrected Christ, He showed His power over death, over the elements, over spirits, and even declared His godly powers to forgive sins, for He had authority and power from His Father to do so.

The Savior of mankind organized His church while He was on earth to provide the saving ordinances, the priesthood authority by which man acts in His name, and as an organized means of carrying out His holy purposes, His ministry among men, which is to continue as long as they are worthy. And as the resurrected Messiah, He appeared to disciples in both the old world and the new, and promised to come again in all His glory.

We Are Christians Because . . .

We Believe in the Basic Principles and Ordinances of the Gospel

"We believe that the first principles and ordinances of the Gospel are: first, Faith in the Lord Jesus Christ; second, Repentance; third, Baptism by immersion for the remission of sins; fourth, Laying on of hands for the gift of the Holy Ghost." (Article of Faith 4.)

Members of The Church of Jesus Christ of Latter-day Saints teach, preach, and observe these very basic principles and ordinances of the gospel, as they were taught by Jesus Christ during His ministry upon the earth some twenty centuries ago.

We believe that because of the Atonement, all mankind will be resurrected as a free gift and that those who believe and obey will also gain eternal life. Thus both immortality and eternal life come to us by His goodness and grace. That obedience which leads to eternal life includes compliance with the basic principles and ordinances of the gospel.

First, Faith in the Lord Jesus Christ

Jesus Christ is the chief cornerstone of our religion, and we teach at every opportunity faith in Him. The Bible teaches that by grace are we saved through faith (Ephesians 2:8); we are all the children of God through faith in Christ (Galatians 3:36); and through faith, we may inherit the promises of the Father (Hebrews 6:12).

The Book of Mormon, which Latter-day Saints believe is another testament of Jesus Christ, is replete with references to

Him and the importance of faith in Him. For example, we learn that—

1. The Lord is able to do all things for us if we exercise faith in Him. (1 Nephi 7:12.)

2. Sins are forgiven because of faith in Him. (Enos 1:8.)

3. Salvation comes through faith on His name. (Mosiah 3:9, 12.)

4. We are given strength according to our faith in Him. (Alma 14:26.)

5. Those who look upon Him with faith will have eternal life. (Helaman 8:15.)

6. Remission of sins comes through Him, by endurance of faith on His name. (Moroni 3:3.)

7. He is the author and finisher of faith. (Moroni 6:4.)

8. If we have faith in Him, we will have power to do whatever is expedient in Him. (Moroni 7:33.)

9. If we ask with faith in Him, He will manifest truth unto us. (Moroni 10:4.)

The Doctrine and Covenants, a collection of revelations to the Church today, gives other examples of the importance of faith in Jesus Christ. The Latter-day Saints are told that they should declare repentance and faith in Him (D&C 19:31), that angels declared redemption to Adam through faith in Him (D&C 29:42), and that parents are obligated to teach faith in Jesus Christ to their children (D&C 68:25).

The wide range of teachings concerning Jesus Christ found in our modern-day scriptures, including the Book of Mormon and Doctrine and Covenants, is demonstrated in the index to those books. Twenty-four headings refer specifically to Jesus Christ, while more than two dozen others describe His role in our doctrines, philosophies, and practices. Included are such subjects as these: Jesus Christ—Advocate; Jesus Christ, Appearances of; Jesus Christ, Atonement through; Jesus Christ, Condescension of; Jesus Christ—Creator; Jesus Christ, Death of; Jesus Christ, First Coming of; Jesus Christ—Good Shepherd; Jesus Christ—Holy One of Israel; Jesus Christ—Immanuel; Jesus Christ—Jehovah; Jesus Christ—Lamb of God; Jesus Christ—Lord; Jesus Christ—Lord of Hosts; Jesus Christ—Mediator; Jesus Christ—

Messiah; Jesus Christ—Only Begotten; Jesus Christ—Redeemer; Jesus Christ, Resurrection of; Jesus Christ—Savior; Jesus Christ, Second Coming of; Jesus Christ—Son of God; Jesus Christ—Son of Man. No other subject comes even close to the space, the emphasis, and the concentration that is given to our beloved Savior. The Book of Mormon is a testament of Him; the Doctrine and Covenants is about Him; the Pearl of Great Price, a third book of modern-day scripture, is about Him; our meetings and our sermons and our ordinances are about Him. All of these scriptures and our teachings emphasize the importance of faith in Him.

Second, Repentance

Repentance is a Christian requirement, but it antedates the Christian era. The prophets of the Old Testament cried repentance to the people. To repent is to change, to forsake one's ways, to abandon that course or those acts that are contrary to the word of God.

Repentance has always been a requirement for baptism into Christ's church. Just as He sent the Twelve Apostles out to preach repentance (see Mark 6:12), so we send missionaries and apostles out to preach repentance today. We do so in a spirit of brotherly love and understanding. We do not hold ourselves up as saintly, but rather as brothers and sisters in the gospel who are striving to work out our own salvation through faith and repentance. The fact that we cry repentance is not judgmental on our part. However, if awareness of sin occurs, if remorse for sin begins to bother the conscience of the hearer, and if that person returns to Christ and departs from the paths of error, that should please all Christendom and benefit society.

Just as the Bible places great emphasis on the importance of repentance, so the modern scriptures are full of words of Christ calling all to repent. In the Book of Mormon we read that men can be found blameless before God only through repentance and faith (Mosiah 3:21); the Lord commands his people to persuade all men to repent (2 Nephi 26:27); only those who repent and confess their sins are numbered among the people of the church (Mosiah 26:35-36); the Lord is given power from the Father to redeem His people because of their repentance (Helaman 5:11); and the Lord will receive all who repent and come unto Him as little children (3 Nephi 9:22).

The Doctrine and Covenants contains revelations in which the Lord commands all men to repent (D&C 18:9, 22, 42); those who do not repent shall lose the light they have received (D&C 1:33), while those who repent and keep His commandments shall be forgiven (D&C 1:32); and to those who repent and sanctify themselves, eternal life shall be given (D&C 133:62).

Christian prophets have always called the world to repentance. In fact, we would have little claim that our prophets are really prophets if they did not call mankind to repent, to change, and to turn to the ways of the Lord.

Third, Baptism by Immersion for the Remission of Sins

We believe in the same baptism and the same mode of baptism as that which was practiced by Jesus Christ, by John the Baptist, and by the early apostles and disciples.

We believe that baptism should be by immersion because that is the way John baptized, and it alone preserves all of the Christian symbolism. He went to a place where the river was deep enough so that he could perform the ordinance in the correct way. In the Gospel of Matthew we read that when Jesus was baptized by John, he "went up straightway out of the water." (Matthew 3:16.) Ancient records and traditions indicate that baptism was by immersion. The Greek word *bapto* means to submerge totally; thus, ancient Greek manuscripts speak of a sunken ship as a "baptized ship." Some of the oldest ruins of early Christian chapels still have a baptismal font that is large enough for both the priest and the initiate.

Early records note the time of the change and even the reason for the change from baptism by immersion to baptism by sprinkling; it was a matter of convenience principally for the elderly and the person who performed the ordinance. We respect the beliefs of those who follow that tradition, but we state our firm belief that the full symbolism of immersion is a very necessary part of a baptism that will be honored by the Lord. The Savior did not authorize any change in the ordinance, and the substitution of sprinkling loses the required symbolism. Immersion is representative of the bodily death and resurrection of the Savior. Paul wrote: "Know ye not, that so many of us as were baptized into Jesus Christ were baptized into his death? Therefore we are buried with him by baptism into death: that like as Christ was raised up from the dead by the glory of the Father, even so we also should walk in newness of life. For if we have been planted together in the likeness of his death, we shall be also in the likeness of his resurrection." (Romans 6:3-5.)

In the Book of Mormon, when the resurrected Savior appeared to the Nephites, he instructed them: "Then shall ye immerse them in the water, and come forth again out of the water." (3 Nephi 11:26.) And in a modern revelation, He taught that those who will come forth in the "resurrection of the just" are those who "received the testimony of Jesus, and believed on his name and were baptized after the manner of his burial, being buried in the water in his name." (D&C 76:50-51.)

Fourth, Laying On of Hands for the Gift of the Holy Ghost

The personal companionship of the Holy Ghost is promised to all who have faith in Christ, who repent of their sins, and who enter into the waters of baptism. John the Baptist said that he baptized "with water unto repentance: but he that cometh after me . . . shall baptize you with the Holy Ghost." (Matthew 3:11.) When Jesus came up out of the water following His baptism, John saw the heavens open and the Spirit of God "descending like a dove, and lighting upon him." (Matthew 3:16.) He taught His disciples that this higher spiritual baptism would take place shortly after He ascended into heaven. In John we read that this would be after Jesus was glorified. (John 7:39.) This promise was fulfilled at the Day of Pentecost for the apostles and for all of the disciples. From then on, new converts to Christ's church received the Holy Ghost by the laying on of hands by those who had authority to perform this ordinance.

In chapter 8 of the Acts of the Apostles we find the interesting account of new converts baptized by Philip in Samaria, but without being given the gift of the Holy Ghost. The apostles Peter and John, who had higher authority, later visited the area and completed the work of Philip. The scripture reads: "When the apostles which were at Jerusalem heard that Samaria had received the word of God, they sent unto them Peter and John: who, when they were come down, prayed for them [those who had been baptized], that they might receive the Holy Ghost: (for as yet he was fallen upon none of them: only they were baptized in the name of the Lord Jesus.) Then laid they [the apostles] their hands on them [the converts], and they received the Holy Ghost." (Acts 8:14-17.)

The nineteenth chapter of Acts has another illustration of this same practice. When Paul found some of John the Baptist's converts who had not heard of the Holy Ghost, he baptized them again, this time in the name of Jesus Christ. "And when Paul had laid his hands upon them, the Holy Ghost came on them." (Acts 19:6.)

The Holy Ghost is a comforter, a consoler, a teacher, a revealer, a sanctifier, a manifestor, an enlightener. It is he who bears witness to all men that God our Father and His Son, Jesus Christ, exist and live.

People change when they receive the Holy Ghost, and miracles frequently accompany this gift. In the scriptures, we see the apostles become much stronger men of faith after they receive the Holy Ghost than they were previously. The Savior also promised that once they had received this gift, they would be able to perform miracles as He had done. This is because the function or mission of the Holy Ghost, the third member of the Godhead, is to enlighten, to strengthen, and to uplift the mind; to sanctify and to purify the soul; to encourage and to inspire to good works; and to reveal the eternal truths of God.

We Believe That Through the Atonement of Christ, All Mankind May Be Saved

The third Article of Faith of The Church of Jesus Christ of Latter-day Saints declares: "We believe that through the Atonement of Christ, all mankind may be saved, by obedience to the laws and ordinances of the Gospel." There is no other way to salvation.

When we speak of salvation, we are speaking of two separate and distinct kinds of salvation:

1. *Salvation from death, which is unconditional and universal.* Adam and Eve opened the way for each mortal to be born and, at the same time, for each to die. Death is just as much a part of the plan of God as is birth. We do not pretend to understand how it is brought about, but we do know that all mankind will be resurrected because Christ opened the way. Until His resurrection, the wicked who died were in a spirit prison. Even the righteous, those who were faithful, were "gathered together in one place." (D&C 138:12.) His resurrection opens the way for *all* persons, both the good and the bad, to be resurrected. That is part of the plan. The scriptures say, "For as in Adam all die, even so in Christ shall all be made alive." (1 Corinthians 15:22.) Since it does not depend upon anything we can do or not do, and since it was made possible by the sacrifice and intervention of Jesus Christ as a perfect being and the very Son of God, unconditional resurrection comes through the grace of Jesus Christ, through His atonement, through His expiation.

2. *Salvation from our own sins, which is conditional and indi-*

vidual. Again, through the atonement of Christ, His expiation, His mediation, it is possible for every person ever born to obtain forgiveness for his sins and to be absolved from the adverse effects of those personal sins. However, this element of salvation is predicated upon individual and personal efforts toward faith in Jesus Christ, repentance of sins, restitution insofar as possible to those who have been damaged by our sins, and continued righteous efforts in Christian living until the very end of our mortal life.

To illustrate this principle, imagine, if you will, a banker lending to a client a sum of money that is protected through a mortgage on the client's property. Then imagine that because of adverse economic conditions, it is impossible for the client to pay when the note comes due. Even the normal grace period is of no help to the borrower. Finally the banker insists that he has to foreclose on the mortgage to pay the debt. The client pleads, "Please have mercy—you must wait longer. I'm doing the best I can." The banker answers, "I am truly sorry, but in all justice I must take your assets and sell them to pay the debt." The client pleads again for mercy—and the banker insists again on justice. Imagine that at this crucial point a relative of the debtor steps forward and asks the banker, "May I pay the debt and obtain the release of the property? Will that satisfy the requirements of justice that you insist upon?" Of course, the banker readily replies, "Yes, justice only requires the payment of the debt. If you pay off the loan, I will release the mortgaged property to you, and the two of you can work out your own arrangement."

In a way, this illustrates the position that the Savior has taken. In some miraculous way He—as the only sinless being on earth, as the Only Begotten Son of God the Father on the earth, and as the one chosen and ordained before the foundation of the earth to be the Savior and Redeemer—paid the debt to satisfy justice for my sins, for your sins, for the sins of everyone. But there is an agreement made between Christ and us, and unless we live up to it, His atonement does not apply to us. He said, "I, God, have suffered these things for all, that they might not suffer if they would repent; but if they would not repent they must suffer even as I." (D&C 19:16-17.)

The effect of Christ's sacrifice is applicable to our sins only if we do what He has asked us to do. He wants us to obey all His laws and ordinances. If we do not obey, we have no promise. He has said, "I, the Lord, am bound when ye do what I say; but when ye do not what I say, ye have no promise." (D&C 82:10.)

Since He made it possible, it is His right to specify and prescribe what He wants us to do. He is going to be the judge of the degree to which we have obeyed Him, and He will reward us accordingly in the resurrection. This is an extremely important point. The scriptures are full of warnings. For example, in Paul's epistle to the Christians at Rome, we read: "God shall judge the secrets of men by Jesus Christ." He tells them that "not the hearers of the law are just before God, but the doers of the law shall be justified." They are to prepare for "the righteous judgment of God, who will render to every man according to his deeds: to them who by patient continuance in well doing seek for glory and honour and immortality, eternal life," which means exaltation. (See Romans 2:16, 13, 6-7.)

One of the most common errors in contemporary theology is the concept that there is only one resurrection. In his first letter to the Corinthians, Paul explains that there will be many different kinds of resurrection. "Christ died for our sins," he said. "Now is Christ risen from the dead, and become the firstfruits of them that slept. For since by man came death, by man came also the resurrection of the dead. For as in Adam all die, even so in Christ shall all be made alive. But every man in his own order." (1 Corinthians 15:3, 20-22.) By order, Paul meant that there would be many different orders of resurrection. He then went on to explain that the resurrection of the dead is as if "there is one glory of the sun, and another glory of the moon, and another glory of the stars: for one star differeth from another star in glory." (1 Corinthians 15:41.) It appears obvious, and agrees with reason as well as with other pronouncements revealed by the prophets, that in the Father's house are many mansions (John 14:2), and the glory of one's resurrection will be appropriate to what one merits through righteous living in this life.

An excellent explanation of this doctrine is found in the writings of Dr. Daniel H. Ludlow, a Latter-day Saint theologian and teacher. He writes:

The law of justice works in relationship to the other laws of God in the moral realm. In essence, the law of justice might be explained as follows: (1) every law has both a punishment and a blessing attached to it; (2) whenever the law is transgressed (broken), a punishment (or suffering) must be inflicted; (3) whenever a law is kept (obeyed), a blessing (or reward) must be given.

The law of justice requires that God must be a God of order and that he must be just and impartial. Because of the law of justice, God can make such statements as these: "I, the Lord, am bound when ye do what I say; but when ye do not what I say, ye have no promise" (Doctrine and Covenants 82:10); "There is a law, irrevocably decreed in heaven before the foundations of this world, upon which all blessings are predicated—And when we obtain any blessing from God, it is by obedience to that law upon which it is predicated" (Doctrine and Covenants 130:20-21).

The law of mercy agrees entirely with the law of justice. However, the law of mercy introduces the possibility of vicarious payment of the laws that have been transgressed. In essence, the law of mercy might be paraphrased as follows: Whenever a law is transgressed (or broken), a payment (or suffering or atonement) must be made; however, the person who transgressed the law does not need to make payment *if* he will repent and *if* he can find someone else who is both able and willing to make payment. Note that the law of mercy insists that the demands of the law of justice be met fully. As Alma stated, ". . . justice exerciseth all his demands, and also mercy claimeth all which is her own; and thus, none but the truly penitent are saved. What, do ye suppose that mercy can rob justice? I say unto you, Nay; not one whit. If so, God would cease to be God." (Alma 42:24-25.)

The law of justice made the atonement of Jesus Christ necessary. When Adam fell, he transgressed a law that had physical and spiritual death as its punishment. Thus the law of justice demanded payment (or atonement) for the broken (or transgressed) law.

The law of mercy made the atonement of Jesus Christ possible. In order for Jesus Christ to pay fully for the law Adam had transgressed, it was necessary that the Savior be both able and willing to make atonement. He was willing to make payment because of his great love for mankind, and he was able to make payment because he lived a sinless life and because he was actually, literally, biologically the Son of God in the flesh. Thus he had the power to atone for the spiritual and physical deaths introduced by the fall of Adam and Eve. Because of this atonement (or payment), he is rightfully referred to as the Savior and Redeemer of all mankind.

Every person benefits unconditionally from two major aspects of the atonement: (1) the resurrection, and (2) the full payment for the original transgression of Adam and Eve. However, as Mosiah indicates, there are also some conditional aspects of the atonement, and in order to benefit from these a person must repent of his sins. Otherwise, "mercy . . . could have claim" upon the person "no more forever," for the law of mercy is made active in the life of a person only upon the conditions of repentance. (Mosiah 3:25-27.) (Daniel H. Ludlow, *A Companion to Your Study of the Book of Mormon,* Salt Lake City: Deseret Book, 1976, pp. 176-77.)

We are Christians because we have faith in and look forward to salvation from temporal death and salvation from spiritual death because of the atonement of Jesus Christ, who paid the price.

We Are Christians Because . . .

We Believe That We Will Be
Judged for Our Own Actions

One of the basic tenets of the Latter-day Saints is expressed in our second Article of Faith: "We believe that men will be punished for their own sins, and not for Adam's transgression."

We fully realize that each of us is responsible and accountable for his own actions, and that we will stand before God to be judged according to our works. (See Revelation 20:12.) We believe that the Savior is pleased with those who do the will of our Father in heaven. (Matthew 7:21.) This Christian principle causes us to seek to live better lives and to seek to accomplish good in the world.

One of the strongest points of doctrine of the original Christians was the concept that Christ atoned for the sins of Adam, just as He has atoned for our sins. It should therefore follow that we are not jeopardized or prejudged because of anything that Adam did. The early Christians sought to live responsibly and never blamed their own weaknesses on anything other than themselves.

The transgression of Adam and Eve in the Garden of Eden was not an accident nor was it even a surprise to our Heavenly Father. We are not in a "Plan B" mode that God had to devise when things went wrong in the garden. On the contrary, this state of mortality is exactly what was supposed to happen. If we think that Eve's eating the forbidden fruit was unplanned, then we doubt the wisdom and infinite foreknowledge of our Creator. The fall was not happenstance. God knew what Satan would do. He knew what Eve would do. And He knew what Adam's reaction would be. The Garden of Eden experience was necessary to accomplish God's plan for us.

Joseph Fielding Smith, tenth president of The Church of Jesus Christ of Latter-day Saints, wrote:

> I never speak of the part Eve took in this fall as a sin, nor do I accuse Adam of a sin. One may say, "Well did they not break a commandment?" Yes. But let us examine the nature of that commandment and the results which came out of it.
>
> In no other commandment the Lord ever gave to man, did he say: "But of the tree of the knowledge of good and evil, thou shalt not eat of it, nevertheless, thou mayest choose for thyself." (Moses 3:17.) . . .
>
> I am sure that neither Adam nor Eve looked upon it as a sin, when they learned the consequences, and this is discovered in their words after they learned the consequences.
>
> Adam said: "Blessed be the name of God, for because of my transgression my eyes are opened, and in this life I shall have joy, and again in the flesh I shall see God."
>
> Eve said: "Were it not for our transgression we never should have had seed, and never should have known good and evil, and the joy of our redemption, and the eternal life which God giveth unto all the obedient." (Moses 5:10-11.)
>
> We can hardly look upon anything resulting in such benefits as being a sin, in the sense in which we consider sin. (*Doctrines of Salvation,* Salt Lake City: Bookcraft, 1954, 1:114-15.)

Some philosophers seem to feel that because of Adam's transgression, every child born into this world has an inclination toward doing evil and that baptism is the only way to overcome this natural bias. As Latter-day Saints, we feel that infants are born innocent of sin, that they cannot sin, and that instead of a tendency toward sin, they remain innocent until the age of accountability, which is eight years of age. From then on, the child can choose between good and evil. One of our prominent authors and philosophers, Dr. David H. Yarn, has written:

> In a modern revelation the Lord said: "Every spirit of man was innocent in the beginning; and God having redeemed man from the fall, men became again, in their infant state, innocent

before God. And that wicked one cometh and taketh away light and truth, through disobedience, from the children of men, and because of the tradition of their fathers." (Doctrine and Covenants 93:38-39.)

Thus, from the beginning of man's mortal existence the wicked one, the devil, has engaged in taking away "light and truth." He has done this through men, individually and collectively—individually through disobedience and collectively through the tradition of their fathers.

Fundamentally, the revelation teaches us that infants are innocent, but that they are born in a mortal world where men are agents unto themselves; where various factors influence decisions; and where, through the exercise of agency, men individually and in varying degrees have chosen to acknowledge or to deny God, to accept and practice His principles or to reject them. Consequently, although babies are innocent, by the time they reach the age of accountability they have become acquainted, through their own weaknesses and those of others, with a fallen world. Although not comprehending these words, they no doubt quite adequately understand that man has his failings. Perhaps this is in part what King Benjamin had in mind when he said:

"For the natural man is an enemy to God, and has been from the fall of Adam, and will be, forever and ever, unless he yields to the enticings of the Holy Spirit, and putteth off the natural man and becometh a saint through the atonement of Christ the Lord, and becometh as a child, submissive, meek, humble, patient, full of love, willing to submit to all things which the Lord seeth fit to inflict upon him, even as a child doth submit to his father." (Mosiah 3:19.)

Other scriptural passages speak of the natural man as carnal, sensual, and devilish. (See Alma 42:10; Moses 5:13.) These words may seem harsh, but it is probably impossible for us even to guess what the corrupt state of man would be had there not been periodic restorations of the Gospel in man's history and some glimmer of spiritual knowledge trickling down through the centuries.

It is important that the teaching of King Benjamin be distinguished from the apostate doctrine of depravity. Man is not born evil, but innocent. He is innocent until he reaches the age of accountability, but he grows up in a world of sin and as an

agent makes choices from among the vast complex of enticements; and when he becomes accountable and refuses to make
his will submissive to God by accepting Him and making covenants with Him, he is "carnal, sensual, and devilish." . . .

Summarily put, the natural man (he who is carnal, sensual,
and devilish, he who is an enemy to God) is the man who has
not humbled himself before God and made covenants with God
by receiving the revealed ordinances at the hands of God's authorized servants; or the man who, having done these things,
has failed to live according to the covenants made in baptism
and to the injunction given when he was confirmed a member of
the Church—"Receive the Holy Ghost." (*Gospel Living in the
Home,* Salt Lake City: Deseret Sunday School Union of The
Church of Jesus Christ of Latter-day Saints, 1962, pp. 50-51.)

I repeat, the early Christians did not blame their human failings on Adam. They accepted their own burden and turned to
Christ, through faith and repentance, for relief from guilt and for
remission of their sins. He paid the price.

We Believe in the Living Christ, Not Graven Images

Latter-day Saints are Christians because, like the early Christians, we worship no graven images. We do not bow down before any statues or icons or paintings, or any manmade representations of anything living or dead. We give no religious importance to medals, relics of ancient times, the cross as the symbol of the dying Christ, nor to burning candles, prayer wheels, beads, or anything designed to help the memory or to become an object of worship in itself.

Let me also state that we respect the rights of all persons to worship their god or gods in their own manner and custom. We even believe this to be a natural and correct and God-given right. We also believe and express the basic philosophy that no man is ever better than when he is in prayer and worship to his God.

Most of Christianity has adopted the cross as a veritable symbol of Christianity, with the implication that if any people do not use the cross on their buildings or inside their chapels or cathedrals, they must not be Christians. We believe that the cross is to be respected as a religious symbol of others, but not as a symbol to *us.* The Lord has commanded: "Thou shalt not make unto thee any graven image, or any likeness of any thing that is in heaven above, or that is in the earth beneath, or that is in the water under the earth. Thou shalt not bow down thyself to them, nor serve them." (Exodus 20:4-5.) Thus, we believe that we have been counseled not to use the cross or other symbols in our worship. We respectfully hope and pray that once this has been explained, our

Christian friends will respect our customs as we do theirs.

To us, the cross is a symbol of His passion, His agony. Our preference is to remember His resurrection. We seek to honor the living Christ who was brought forth in glory from the tomb on the third day. We remember Him appearing to Mary Magdalene, to Peter, and to the two disciples on the road to Emmaus, and to the group of Christians gathered in the upper chambers with doors and windows closed to avoid persecution from the Jews. We remember Him resurrected and glorified, having overcome death. We see Him as a strong, masculine, healthy Savior of mankind, not an emaciated and suffering one.

We believe that the way we worship is more important than the physical symbols used in worship. An example of this is found in the experience of two tourists who were attending the weekly broadcast of the Mormon Tabernacle Choir in the Salt Lake Tabernacle. One of them remarked to the other, "I told you they are not Christians. Look—there isn't a cross anywhere to be seen!" The other whispered back, "But didn't you hear the prayer they offered before they started? It was all a straight Christian prayer. The man even ended saying 'In the name of our Lord, Jesus Christ.'"

On Temple Square in Salt Lake City, in some of our visitors centers, and at many of our historical landmarks, one will find beautiful statues. For example, on the top spire of some of our temples is a gold-plated statue of the Angel Moroni, who appeared to the Prophet Joseph Smith and revealed to him the location of the plates on which were engraved the message of the Book of Mormon. We do not worship that statue nor look upon it in a religious way. It is a decoration only, a representation in art of the message of the restoration of Christ's gospel in our time. Another example is the statue of the *Christus* in the visitors center on Temple Square, a magnificent marble statue carved by Danish artist Bertel Thorvaldsen. In the grounds of the square are statues that represent the restoration of the Aaronic Priesthood in our dispensation; the miracle of the seagulls that devoured the crickets and helped save the crops of the early settlers in the Salt Lake Valley; the valiant handcart pioneers; and other historic events. Again, no religious significance is attributed to these statues. They are only representational, reminders of our heritage.

In my home I have several statues. One is a three-foot bronze of a bearded man in a frock coat, a book in his left hand, with his right hand raised in a gesture typical of someone preaching a fervent sermon. When I bought it in South America, I thought the man looked very much like my great-grandfather as a missionary, preaching about the Book of Mormon. One much-treasured work of art is a life-size bust of Joseph Smith that was carved by a Latter-day Saint in Ecuador. I feel that it is the finest portrayal of the Prophet I have ever seen. But none of these items receives the slightest religious attention; they are appreciated as fine artwork only.

In the name of our church is the word *saints*. Some think that we therefore worship "saints," prophets or other worthy persons who have been canonized. The definition of the word *saint* that I like best is "one who has made a covenant with the Lord." We do not worship saints or statues of saints from either ancient or modern times. Rather, we consider all members of The Church of Jesus Christ of Latter-day Saints to be persons who have covenanted with the Lord through baptism and who have therefore become followers of Christ.

This interpretation is consistent with the teachings of the early Christian church. The apostle Paul referred to all of the early disciples of Christ as "saints." He wrote to "the saints which are at Ephesus," "all the saints in Christ Jesus which are at Philippi," "the saints and faithful brethren in Christ which are at Colosse," and "the church of God which is at Corinth, to them that are sanctified in Christ Jesus, called to be saints." Although no member of the Church today pretends to be saintly, all have the goal of progressing steadily toward perfection, since that is a commandment of the Lord: "Be ye therefore perfect, even as your Father which is in heaven is perfect." (Matthew 5:45.) Those who are members of the Church have every right to consider themselves saints of the latter days. We use the term "latter days" to differentiate between the time of Christ (former days) and today (the latter days).

In keeping with our concern to not offend the Lord by having "other gods" or "graven images," we are also careful about the way we look upon the mother of our Savior. We believe in the miracle of the virgin birth. We love and honor Mary, the mother of Christ. She is even mentioned in the Book of Mormon by Christian prophets in the Americas before the meridian of time. Six centuries before the birth of Jesus, Nephi saw her in a vision. Another prophet, who lived about one century before Jesus' birth, was instructed by an angel and told what the name of the Son of God would be and what would be the name of His mother. (See Mosiah 3:8.) Nevertheless, we do not worship Mary, nor do we pray to her. In fact, we feel that the scriptures are quite specific in declaring that only the Savior is an intermediary between man and God the Father: "No man cometh unto the Father, but by me." (John 14:6.)

In our meetinghouses as well as many of our homes, you will find pictures of prophets or past leaders of the Church, biblical or Book of Mormon scenes, and also paintings of the Savior. Often you will find a painting showing the first vision of Joseph Smith, when God the Father and His Son, Jesus Christ, appeared to the youth in the Sacred Grove. But again, these are regarded only as artwork; they are not part of any religious worship or service.

These beliefs are explained only to help the reader understand our traditions and are not meant as criticism of the traditions and beliefs of others. Every man is at his best when approaching the deity he worships. We desire to be respectful of anything that is important to any other child of our Heavenly Father. We pray that all others will allow us the same privilege.

We Are Christians Because . . .

We Believe in Honoring
the Name of the Lord

We are Christians because, like the early Christians, we do not take the name of the Lord in vain, nor do we allow the misuse of any terms referring even obliquely to Deity. We believe that anyone who professes to be a follower of Christ would not use vulgar expressions or common four-letter vulgarities and especially would not use in an improper way any expression reserved for Deity.

In our pursuit of all that is Christian, we earnestly seek to avoid all things that are in effect anti-Christ or non-Christian. We feel strongly that using the names of Deity in a profane and vulgar way is offensive to our Heavenly Father and to our Savior, and is contrary to all that they represent.

The third of the Ten Commandments states: "Thou shalt not take the name of the Lord thy God in vain; for the Lord will not hold him guiltless that taketh his name in vain." (Exodus 20:7.) This commandment is well known to the entire Christian world; yet even in predominantly Christian countries we observe frequent abuse of all that is sacred, tender, holy, and spiritual to those who truly believe in Christ. It is frightening that even in areas that pretend to be Christian and to follow Christian traditions, the misuse of sacred names and terminology is so prevalent. To the ears of one who understands and observes this commandment, such oaths and vulgar expressions are painful to hear.

In years gone by, only those who were low and uncultured would dare to use profanity, and the names of and references to Deity were reserved for sacred occasions of worship and prayer.

Women and children were considered special, and language was controlled and softened in their presence. Today it seems as though Satan has control of the tongues of many youths and adults—both men and women—in our society.

In The Church of Jesus Christ of Latter-day Saints, we teach respect for and proper use of the sacred words and terms and names that are, in our opinion, holy and hallowed. We feel that it is a responsibility of parents to control their own tongues and to set a proper example for their children. We feel that the true Christian would never let improper or unseemly words escape his lips. We teach, preach, correct, train, and emphasize the development of a proper vocabulary to express oneself rather than allowing lapses into base and ugly words or vulgar abuse of the names of those whom we worship, God the Father and His Son, Jesus Christ. We feel that our language at work and at play, in the home and in the community, and wherever we may be, should be the same as that which we would use in church.

Even in extreme frustration, it is possible to find more eloquent words to express oneself than vulgarities or profanities. A good illustration of such self-control is found in the true experience of a prominent Church leader and a high-ranking governmental leader who once played a round of golf together. On one hole the Church leader positioned the ball, drew his club back, and swung—and muffed the shot. As he saw the ball go into the rough, he stared at it in complete silence. Finally the political leader commented, "Anyone else would have sworn." The Church leader replied, "I never swear, but where I spit, the grass will never grow!" How much more powerful is such an expression than an angry stream of profanities!

Another story is told about Spencer W. Kimball, president and prophet of The Church of Jesus Christ of Latter-day Saints. As he was being rolled into an operating room on a gurney, the orderly pushing the bed smashed his finger between the door frame and the bed frame. Immediately he cursed, taking the name of the Lord in vain. President Kimball, his senses already dulled somewhat from the anesthesia, opened his eyes and said quietly to the orderly, "Young man, please don't say that. Jesus is my best friend."

Do you and I have the courage to stand up for the Savior and request that His name not be used in a vulgar way to express pain? Do we have the strength of our convictions to ask that the name of our Father in heaven not be used improperly, nor any other common expressions?

There are several kinds of profanity. First, there are those expressions in which the names of Deity are used. This includes expressions that are derivatives of the names of Deity, such as "jeez," "gol," and so forth. We find offense in both the title of Deity being used in a profane manner and the shortened or adulterated versions.

One of our children's teachers was using the name of the Lord in almost every sentence as the students brought out her impatience. It was offensive to many of the students and was brought to our attention. When we visited with her to ask that she control her tongue, she replied, "I'm only asking the Lord for help when I use His name." I do not believe she was aware that there is a big difference between an honest prayer and a use so frequent that the sacred title is profaned.

Another kind of profanity is a group of four-letter words that are commonly used in anger, frustration—and even, sad to say, everyday speech. They are a cheap substitute for an inadequate vocabulary, and there is no excuse for their use by Christians who know better and who are adult enough to think before using them. Such words should never be used in anger, never in frustration, never habitually, and never in an inappropriate situation where any might take offense.

Extremely offensive to the true Christian—and indeed, to any sensitive and intelligent person—are profanities that derive from bathroom filth and from sexual implications. Only the most immature and uncouth person would use such expressions, which, unfortunately, are becoming more common in everyday speech as well as in movies, on television, and in books. It is inconceivable that anyone using such words and expressions as part of his personality and vocabulary could ever hope to approach our Heavenly Father. The Lord can never be pleased with such use of the tongue and mind of man.

The Savior said, "Let your communication be, Yea, yea; Nay,

nay." (Matthew 5:37.) In other words, to be truly Christian, we must control our words, and to do that, we must control our thoughts. As the prophet Alma said, "Our words will condemn us, . . . and our thoughts will also condemn us." (Alma 12:14.) It is wrong even to have improper thoughts. If we control ourselves, we will control our thoughts and our words, and then our actions will also please the Lord.

We Are Christians Because . . .

We Believe in the Same Organization as Existed in the Primitive Church

The sixth Article of Faith of The Church of Jesus Christ of Latter-day Saints states: "We believe in the same organization that existed in the Primitive Church, namely, apostles, prophets, pastors, teachers, evangelists, and so forth."

One of the distinguishing features of the Church is that we believe in the same priesthood structure as existed in the early Church of Christ: the Aaronic Priesthood, with the offices of deacon, teacher, priest, and bishop; and the Melchizedek Priesthood, with the offices of elder, seventy, high priest, patriarch, and apostle. The priesthood administers as well as carries out the sacred ordinances required for salvation, such as baptism by immersion, the bestowal of the Holy Ghost by the laying on of hands, the sacrament of the Lord's Supper, ordination to the priesthood, marriage, and sacred ordinances performed in our temples.

In his epistle to the Ephesians, Paul states that Christ "gave some, apostles; and some, prophets; and some, evangelists; and some, pastors and teachers." Then he explains why the priesthood and its various offices were organized: (1) "for the perfecting of the saints," that is, those members of the Church who believe in Christ, not persons considered to be sanctified or perfected already; (2) "for the work of the ministry"; and (3) "for the edifying of the body of Christ," that is, the building up of the Church, "till we all come in the unity of the faith." (Ephesians 4:11-12.)

When any organization grows significantly or circumstances

change dramatically, it is normal to expect a minor change in the administrative structure. Moses handled things well when he led the hundreds of thousands of Israelites out of Egypt, but in the desert the administrative load was so heavy that his father-in-law had to point out to him the need to delegate to other levels much of the routine work. However, we feel that, as Christians, we have every right to expect that the same basic structure and offices and system of administration set in place by the Savior will continue to exist and even be a standard one might use to identify the true Christian church. The ordinances themselves would also be a required standard of measurement to identify how closely a particular church adheres to that which was established by the Savior and His apostles when they were on earth.

Some major parts of the scriptures found in the Bible are missing. Over the centuries translators and scribes left many essential parts out, either because they did not know how to translate them or because there was a significant difference between the practice of their day and that which was stated in the scriptures. So, rather than let the difference be visible, they decided to leave the discrepancy out. Among those items that apparently were not explained fully are the offices and functions of the priesthood, as well as the ordinances. The serious student may want to investigate these things for himself; however, through the ancient scriptures and those that have been revealed in modern times, including the Book of Mormon and the Doctrine and Covenants, the Latter-day Saints have established the priesthood according to the pattern originally established by the Savior.

The *Aaronic Priesthood* is named after Aaron, the brother of Moses, who was appointed to be the spokesman for Moses. Aaron and his sons and descendants were called and set apart to carry out specific priesthood duties. At a later time in history the entire tribe of Levi, one of the twelve tribes, was called to handle some of these duties. This priesthood of Aaron, or Aaronic Priesthood, which is also called the Levitical Priesthood, is referred to in the scriptures. It encompasses the offices of deacon, teacher, priest, and bishop. It holds the keys of the ministering of angels, which means that a person who has this priesthood can, acting appropriately, open the door to receive visits and/or help from angels on

the other side of the veil. It also holds the keys of the gospel of repentance and baptism by immersion for the remission of sins.

At one time the priesthood was passed down in ancient Israel
from father to son, but it was later changed to a merit basis. The
matter of appropriate ages has also changed over the centuries.
Today, young men and new converts to the Church generally hold
these offices, as part of their training for the Melchizedek Priesthood. As a rule, a deacon is ordained at age twelve, a teacher at
age fourteen, and a priest at age sixteen, depending, of course,
upon individual worthiness.

The *Melchizedek Priesthood* is named after Melchizedek, the
king of Salem, a great high priest about whom little is known except that he was highly favored of the Lord and even received
tithes from Abraham. This priesthood includes all other offices
not mentioned in the Aaronic Priesthood, such as elder, seventy, high priest, patriarch, and apostle. Those who hold these
positions are responsible for presiding, supervising, leading, and
blessing. They administer spiritual matters, with the privilege of
having the heavens opened to them for guidance in their callings.

The basic leadership structure of the Church is through councils or quorums. The First Presidency, the presiding quorum, consists of the prophet, who is president of the Church and the presiding high priest, and his two counselors, also high priests.

The Quorum of the Twelve Apostles, also designated as the
Council of the Twelve, is comprised of high priests who have been
called to be special witnesses of Christ to all the world. They may
officiate in all of the sacred ordinances, and they travel throughout
the world regulating the affairs of the Church, just as the apostles
of old did. When the First Presidency is dissolved through the
death of the president, the authority to direct church government reverts at once to the Quorum of the Twelve Apostles. The
president of the Twelve, who is the high priest with greatest
longevity as a member of the quorum, directs the affairs of the
Church and reorganization of the presidency, in council with all of
the apostles. According to the pattern established in the Church,
he becomes president and calls two counselors to assist him. Thus,
it is an orderly system completely independent of any political influence. It responds to the will of the Lord as He moves people on

to the next life as He sees fit, or extends life according to His holy purposes. An apostle continues to serve until death, dependent, of course, upon personal worthiness.

The First Quorum of the Seventy is another council that works under the direction of the First Presidency and the Quorum of the Twelve Apostles. Members of this quorum are charged directly with supervising missionary work as well as ecclesiastical matters in various geographical areas assigned to them individually by the Twelve. They also hold administrative and staff positions in the headquarters of the Church. Their specific calling is to (1) preach the gospel, (2) be special witnesses of Christ, (3) build up the Church, and (4) regulate the affairs of the Church. A member of this quorum serves for a designated period or until health considerations cause him to be placed on emeritus status.

The Presiding Bishopric, which supervises temporal matters, consists of the Presiding Bishop and two counselors. They serve under the direction of the First Presidency and the Twelve.

The First Presidency, the Twelve, the Seventy who comprise the First Quorum of the Seventy, and the Presiding Bishopric are all considered to be General Authorities of the Church.

Wherever the Saints are found in sufficient numbers, they are organized into stakes (similar to a diocese), with each stake consisting of several wards or branches (similar to a parish). Three high priests—a president and two counselors—preside over each stake, assisted by twelve high priests who form a "high council." Three high priests—a bishop and two counselors—also preside over a ward, while a branch is governed by a president and two counselors.

Other presiding officers are called as needed, including mission presidents, who generally serve for a period of three years; temple presidents; regional representatives, who counsel and advise regions, or groups of stakes, and so on.

Yes, we believe that Christ organized His church when He was on the earth, and that the same organization exists in His church on the earth today. The two priesthoods, which existed anciently as well as in the early church, have been restored again in their full and official manner, with legal authority to act in the name of God here on earth.

We Believe That One Must Be Called of God, by Those in Authority

Our fifth Article of Faith declares: "We believe that a man must be called of God, by prophecy, and by the laying on of hands by those who are in authority, to preach the Gospel and administer in the ordinances thereof." We also believe that a call to the ministry is something that "no man taketh . . . unto himself," but that he must be "called of God, as was Aaron." (Hebrews 5:4.)

We believe that no person should volunteer himself to occupy an ecclesiastical position as minister or pastor or priest, nor do we believe that an ecclesiastical leader should be paid a salary or fee for preaching the gospel and tending to the flock.

We are well aware that in many Christian churches, a person of either sex may choose to follow the career of the ministry, and that, with appropriate education and training, that person can be duly ordained and offer himself or herself to serve a congregation as a salaried professional. One minister of whom I am aware changed denominations several times in his career when another Christian denomination offered him a better salary. His justification was that the doctrines of the different churches differed only slightly, and it was easy to adapt his sermons accordingly. We respect such flexibility, although we do not really understand it, and we pray that other religions will respect our position even if they do not understand our inflexibility in regard to this matter.

We do not have a professional clergy who have trained and studied for the ministry in the traditional way. Our local leaders are competent in their daily professions from which they earn a living as well as competent as religious leaders through many years of study of the scriptures, church doctrines, and church procedures. Most have served in many ecclesiastical positions and callings, thus acquiring "on-the-job training." All of the local officers are expected to have their own source of income to support adequately their families on the standards they themselves choose. Some are in humble circumstances while others are more affluent. However, this makes no difference in their respective callings. Frequently a humble tradesman will preside over a wealthy financier. There is a parallel, however, between success in one's chosen profession and callings to positions in the church. Logically, a church leader needs all the talent and ability he can possess to meet the challenges of providing spiritual leadership to others, and quite frequently that is found in a person who has been successful in his own work. (I use the masculine pronoun only to avoid awkwardness of saying "he or she." Women also serve in many capacities in the Church and are highly qualified to do so.)

We believe that in order to serve in the Church, a person must be called of God, but please note that we say "called of God by prophecy and by the laying on of hands, by those who are in authority." In other words, we do not consider it correct procedure— nor was it the tradition of the early Christian church—for a person to announce that he feels he has been called of God to go into "the ministry." Christ stated very clearly, "Ye have not chosen me, but I have chosen you." (John 15:16.) We feel that such decisions should be left in the hands of those who are appointed to call others under inspiration from the Lord.

In The Church of Jesus Christ of Latter-day Saints, no one should be ambitious or seek to be called to a position. Of course, all members should be worthy and prepared to accept any callings extended to them. The person who is called responds out of a sense of duty and service and love, and those whom he serves recognize that the service is given with no thought of self. At the same time, under this lay system of service, a person accepts a release just as graciously as he accepts a call. It is just as much a credit to be released honorably as it is to be called to serve.

We believe that responsibilities in the Church should be rotated among a congregation so that most, if not all, have opportunities to serve. This makes ours a church of participants rather than a church of observers.

We believe that inspiration is given to those who are responsible to issue calls to positions in the Church. I had the privilege of seeing such inspiration and feeling its power while on an assignment with President Spencer W. Kimball, our prophet. At the time he was a member of the Twelve and I had just been called to serve as a regional representative of the Council of the Twelve Apostles. He asked me to accompany him on an assignment to select a new president to preside over a stake.

As we drove to the stake center, President Kimball explained what he wanted me to do. He planned to interview a large number of qualified men, including those who were on the stake high council, all the bishops in that stake, outstanding priesthood quorum leaders, and others who were recommended by the outgoing stake presidency. He asked me to keep brief notes on each person interviewed so that he could review the notes later.

As the interviews proceeded throughout the afternoon and into the evening, I wondered how President Kimball would be able to select the new president. Every individual he interviewed seemed to be eminently qualified. All had served faithfully in many Church callings; all were successful in their professions; all were faithful husbands and fathers; all were full tithe payers and kept all the commandments faithfully. It seemed to me that every single individual would make a good stake president.

Then, as President Kimball was asking the usual questions of one particular individual, the impression came to me very strongly, *This man is the new stake president.* I looked up from my note taking and observed that he appeared to be very similar to all the others; there was no sudden flash of light or glow. So I went back to taking notes. Then it came again, that distinct impression that this man was the next stake president. Again I looked, but I saw no visible indication that there was anything different about this man. However, I marked that man's name in my notes with three tiny asterisks.

When President Kimball finished the interview, he indicated that he would like a brief break. Then he came over to me and said, "Bob, did you feel that?" I then knew that he had felt the same sensation that I had felt, and my eyes filled with tears of recognition. He nodded and added, "It usually isn't that strong. Sometimes we have to interview everyone a second time to find the one whom the Lord has prepared. Other times we ask if there is a 'David' out tending the flocks that we might have overlooked. But this time the inspiration was so strong that I thought even you might have felt it." I will always treasure that moment with a prophet who received inspiration so strong that even I felt it.

Several years ago, when I was serving as president of one of our Spanish-speaking missions, one of the Church's apostles came to our mission to help select a priesthood leader for one of our districts. For two days he interviewed various candidates but no decision was made. Then, at the end of our last meeting on Sunday afternoon, members of the congregation filed past the apostle to shake his hand and speak to him through a translator. As one of the men passed by and greeted him in Spanish, the apostle turned to me and said quietly, "There is your man. Who is he?" I had to confess that I did not know the man, and I asked a person standing nearby who he was. The apostle, however, under the influence of the Spirit, had picked out the only man in the congregation who had had prior Church leadership experience that would qualify him for the position in question; in addition, this was the only man who had a telephone and adequate transportation. He was successful in his profession and a devoted family man.

There is work enough for all; no one need be left out. All calls are given by inspiration, and it is a very spiritual experience to see new leaders called when others are released.

Inspiration occurs at all levels in the Church. Each person is entitled to seek and to receive inspiration to help him fulfill his callings. Guidelines and instruction manuals are prepared on a churchwide basis, providing for uniformity in our programs, but each person can call upon the Lord for additional inspiration to help him magnify his calling. The Sunday School teacher may be inspired to add one more illustration from the scriptures to her lesson, and that might trigger a reaction in a student. "You surely were inspired," the student says. "That scripture answered a question I have had for a long time. How did you know what I needed?" Of course, no one knows the answer except to say, "The Lord loves you—He knows what you needed to hear, and He prompted me to add it to my lesson."

In one of our wards, the bishop needed to call a new counselor to replace one who had moved away. There were several worthy men in the congregation, but the Spirit kept prompting the bishop with the name of a man who was timid in public and who had never held a leadership position in the Church. The bishop discussed these promptings with the stake president, and the president's counsel was that if the spiritual feelings persisted after the bishop had fasted and prayed, he should call the man even if it seemed contrary to "worldly wisdom." The man was called, and he accepted the call with fear and trembling. But the Lord made him equal to the task. His ability to conduct meetings and speak in public gradually improved. His natural humility was an asset as he served with others who were high-powered, goal-oriented executives. He was able to personally reach many inactive church members and bring them back into the fold.

But the biggest miracle was an intimate and special one. The man's wife had never before seen any leadership qualities in her husband. But from the moment he was called to serve in the bishopric, she began to see him in new light. Their marriage was greatly improved by this call. They had a rebellious teenage son who had never exhibited much admiration or respect for his father. That changed the day his girl friend casually remarked, "My parents think your dad is the best second counselor we have ever had in our bishopric."

In the mission field, mission presidents often face situations no one could possibly have anticipated and for which they could not possibly have been given advance counsel and warning. With from one hundred to two hundred missionaries to supervise, as well as the problems of branches that often have few experienced leaders and many inactive persons to reactivate, the mission president is faced every day with enormous challenges. No one can handle this kind of job on the basis of talent alone. Too many lives are involved. Only inspiration from the Lord can do it. The rewards and blessings come in reports from those whose lives are changed as a result of a new calling or a new mission assignment or a new companion. One missionary wrote to his president, "You surely were inspired to send me to this city. You could not have known that I had seen it in a dream before my mission. Now I know the Lord is guiding you and that He planned long ago for me to serve in this mission."

These are some of the rewards of those who serve in the Church of Jesus Christ. Hundreds of thousands of leaders and teachers can testify to having received similar inspiration in their callings in the Lord's work. And as these individuals are released from their current callings and receive new ones, as a result of the lay ministry of the Church, they are entitled to inspiration in their new callings. The Lord knows what they need—and He is there to prompt and guide them!

We Are Christians Because . . .

We Believe in Prophets and in Continuing Revelation

As Christians, members of The Church of Jesus Christ of Latter-day Saints believe "all that God has revealed, all that He does now reveal, and we believe that He will yet reveal many great and important things pertaining to the Kingdom of God." (Article of Faith 9.)

We believe in prophets and in the principle of continuing revelation in our day, "as well in these times as in times of old, and as well in times of old as in times to come." (1 Nephi 10:19.) We are convinced that the love of Christ extends to all who have lived, who do live, and who will yet live on the earth, and that He is our Shepherd today as well as anciently. And because He loves us, He sends prophets to the world today as He did in the past.

Our first message to the world is that Christ is the divine Son of God the Father and that salvation comes in and through Him. Our second message is that there are prophets on the face of the earth again, and that Joseph Smith was the first prophet of this dispensation. His divine mission was to declare to the world that the Father and the Son appeared to him in the spring of 1820 with a message for him and for the world. That great vision is the origin of this worldwide Christian faith.

What is a prophet? Here are some of a prophet's attributes, as explained in the scriptures:

1. A prophet talks of Christ, rejoices in Christ, preaches of

Christ, prophesies of Christ, and testifies of Christ, the Messiah, the Son of God.

2. A prophet foresees the future, understands the past, interprets the will of God, warns against sin, teaches eternal truths, defends the faith.

3. A prophet does not need special training in debate, rhetoric, public speaking, elocution, or philosophic argument in order to present his divine message.

4. A prophet boldly declares that God has spoken to him.

5. A prophet has overcome sin in his life. He keeps himself pure in order to receive the Spirit.

6. A prophet agrees with other prophets concerning the doctrines of Christ, though each may be speaking in different centuries, places, or cultures.

7. A prophet is a dignified man with a dignified message; there is no hint of clairvoyance or the supernatural.

8. A prophet is not concerned with making concessions to public opinion or an impression on the public. He stands steadfast in his declarations of truth.

9. A prophet declares his message with directness, without fear, and without argument, concessions, justification, or appeasement to tradition.

10. A prophet does not build up a case by formal argument with an accumulation of evidence; rather, he testifies and states, "Thus saith the Lord."

11. A prophet does not ask people to believe him. Rather, he tests them.

12. A prophet is not swayed by public opinion or what others may think of him.

13. A prophet declares messages that are for his own time and that stand for future times.

14. A prophet receives his call from God, a call that is not transferable to any other person.

15. A prophet declares what God reveals to him.

16. A prophet sees clearly, while others may see in half shadows and fog, if at all.

17. A prophet can endure persecution and will even give his life, if necessary, in defending truth.

18. A prophet denounces sin and wickedness, without fear, wherever he sees it.

19. A prophet does not subscribe to creeds worked out laboriously by councils representing compromises or popular concepts. He follows the pure teachings of Christ and His gospel.

20. A prophet recognizes scholars for what they are, but seldom do scholars recognize him for what he is. Many so-called intellectuals find it inconceivable to acquire knowledge other than by their own methods. They do not usually admit to the workings of the Spirit. They say, "I have never seen a vision; therefore Joseph Smith could not have seen one."

21. A prophet does not try to make the Church, its doctrines, or its philosophies conform to mere intellectual standards. Rather, he teaches the truths as they are, pure and unadulterated.

22. A prophet sees the premortal life, mortality, and life after death as one orderly whole, whereas others usually see only one brief scene, and that with a distorted view.

23. A prophet explains matters in terms of covenants made with God before the foundation of this earth, covenants that lead to a continuation of covenants made in this mortal existence and which, in turn, affect our condition in the life to come.

24. A prophet is willing to give up his own life rather than deny his witness. Paul said, "I saw a light and heard a voice," and his enemies tried to kill him for blasphemy. Stephen said, "I see the heavens opened, and the Son of man standing on the right hand of God," and he was stoned to death. Joseph Smith said, "I saw two Personages, whose brightness and glory defy all description," and he was martyred.

25. A prophet relies on revelation and not on tradition.

Dr. Jeffrey M. Holland, president of Brigham Young University, was once invited to attend a meeting in the Holy Land where a group of Christians, Muslims, and Jews discussed their faith and beliefs. In his presentation, he pointed out that the Jews expected no prophets after the destruction of their temple; the Christians expected no prophets after the book of Revelation; and the Muslims expected no prophets after the death of Mohammed. Then he pointed out that all three groups expected a Messiah. His explanation of how Latter-day Saints fit in with other religions is found in this statement: "You gentlemen ought to know that we believe the process of the coming of the Messiah has begun, and with it the return of prophets and modern revelation."

Yes, we believe in revelation, in "all that God has revealed, all that He does now reveal, and . . . that He will yet reveal many great and important things pertaining to the Kingdom of God." And we believe that these revelations will be revealed through His servants, His prophets!

We Are Christians Because . . .

We Believe in Those Scriptures
Which Testify of Christ

As Latter-day Saints, "we believe the Bible to be the word of God as far as it is translated correctly; we also believe the Book of Mormon to be the word of God." (Article of Faith 8.) We believe those scriptures written by inspired prophets which testify that Jesus Christ is the Son of God and our Savior and Redeemer. This includes the scriptures in the Bible as well as the Book of Mormon, which is a new witness of Jesus Christ. Just as the Bible was written by prophets of God in the old world, so the Book of Mormon was written by prophets in the new world.

The Bible

Latter-day Saints recognize the Bible as the foremost of their standard works and the first among the books of scripture declared to be our written guides in faith, doctrine, ordinances, and commandments. We believe, however, that over the centuries there have been many handmade copyings of the ancient source documents and many translations by different translators. In the process, some things have been left out of the Bible and other things have been changed from their original meaning. We do not hold the Lord accountable for the errors and omissions of men, but simply mention this as fact. We love the Bible and its teachings, and we use it constantly in our meetings and for private study. It is an inspired source of strength and a builder of faith. It is the word of God to His children.

We are concerned that in many so-called Christian homes and

even Christian churches, study and use of the Bible seem to have diminished. Daily scripture reading is an unsurpassed source of peace of mind in this troubled world, and as literature, the Bible is magnificent. But even more, the Old Testament prophesies concerning the coming of the Messiah and tells about the relationship between God and man, while the New Testament tells of the life and miracles of the Savior; His very words are there. When it is read prayerfully, the Spirit bears witness to the reader that these things really happened. The personality and nature of the Son of God become real, and one feels closer to Him and comes to love Him. The four Gospels are especially inspiring with regard to the life of Christ, while the other books of the New Testament serve to show how the early Christians lived, worshiped, preached, thought, and felt about the gospel.

We admire and respect other great religious books that have been written or preserved with the purpose of helping humanity, but we only canonize those words written by Christian prophets that testify of the divine Sonship of Jesus Christ.

The Book of Mormon

Like the Bible, the Book of Mormon is a divinely inspired record. It is a collection of writings left by prophets of many centuries ago who lived in the western hemisphere and who believed in Christ, who prophesied of Christ, and who associated with Him during the brief time He visited them after His crucifixion.

These ancient prophets wrote their history and teachings of Christ laboriously by engraving characters on thin plates of hammered gold. These writings were passed from prophet to prophet, generation to generation, down through the centuries. These are the spiritual records of some—not all—of the people who lived in the western hemisphere. They chronicle the main group of peoples who lived in what are now the Americas from about 600 B.C. to A.D. 400. The last of these peoples lapsed into apostasy at that time, and, according to Moroni, the last prophet who wrote in the record, the Lord withdrew his blessings and the people were exterminated by their enemies.

Moroni hid the gold plates containing the religious history of his people in a stone box on the side of a hill that he called

Cumorah. They were to be handed over to a later generation. In the wisdom of the Lord, that happened on September 22, 1827, when the prophet-writer Moroni returned to earth as a resurrected being to give the history to a new prophet, Joseph Smith. That young prophet was also given divine power from on high to translate the language, unknown to him, into English.

The record, which would be called the Book of Mormon, has an unusual literary style not unlike the New Testament. This would be logical, both because the original authors were also prophets and because Joseph Smith was himself a student of the Bible. He would thus phrase the sacred writings in the traditional King James language, since the concepts were revealed to him by the Spirit. After the gold plates were fully translated, they were taken back by the ancient prophet Moroni.

This remarkable story can be tested from many different viewpoints. For example, Joseph Smith was not the only person who saw the plates. Eleven other persons were allowed to see them, heft them, and note the unusual characters engraven upon them. Three of those persons saw the angel and also heard a voice from heaven declaring that the translation had been done by the gift and power of God and that it was true and correct. They all signed sworn legal affidavits to their experiences, as firsthand witnesses. There is no reason to doubt the history of the origin of the Book of Mormon. Joseph Smith did not pretend to have written it; he only said that the Lord had guided him in the translation.

Today, with modern techniques of analyzing writing style through computers and study of word patterns, it is well established that there are many different styles of authorship in the Book of Mormon, each corresponding to the different prophet-authors named in the book. Thus, no man would have been able to claim to be the sole author. Likewise, the internal construction and pattern attributed to each individual author stand intact, as an integral whole.

The name of the book requires an explanation. It might well have been named the "Book of Moroni" after the last author, the man who delivered the plates to Joseph Smith. It might also have been called very appropriately "Ancient American Writings about Jesus Christ" or "What Prophets on the American Continent

Wrote about Christ." The only thing we really know is that the Lord himself designated the title to be the Book of Mormon, apparently (but not necessarily) because the principal compiler of the final record was the prophet Mormon, father of Moroni. Mormon's assignment was both to write his own record and to condense, under the Spirit, more voluminous works of other authors into the compact version he gave his son Moroni. Thus, the book today is known as the Book of Mormon.

The Book of Mormon contains about one thousand direct references to Christ, the Lamb of God, Redeemer, and other names by which the Son of God has been known. It also has a fifth "Gospel," which complements the four Gospels in the Bible, Matthew, Mark, Luke, and John. This fifth witness is the book of Third Nephi, which relates a visit of Christ to the western hemisphere after His resurrection. It is a fascinating account worthy of the study of every Christian and especially every student of Christian scriptures. This personal visit of the Savior is most certainly the origin of the virtually universal belief of Indians in North and South America that a white, bearded God visited their forefathers and then ascended to heaven with the promise that He would return again. This tradition of a white God probably contributed to the relatively easy conquest of the Americas by the European conquistadors, for the Indian nations apparently attributed divinity to the white man.

The Book of Mormon was brought forth, as is stated in the foreword, "to the convincing of the Jew and Gentile that Jesus is the Christ, the Eternal God." A prophet named Nephi makes strong statements such as these: "We believe in Christ . . . and look forward with steadfastness unto Christ. . . . We talk of Christ, we rejoice in Christ, we preach of Christ, we prophesy of Christ, and we write according to our prophecies, that our children may know to what source they may look for a remission of their sins. Wherefore, we . . . look forward unto that life which is in Christ."

He then ends his statement with these words: "And now behold, I say unto you that the right way is to believe in Christ, and deny him not; and Christ is the Holy One of Israel; wherefore ye must bow down before him, and worship him with all your might, mind, and strength, and your whole soul; and if ye do this ye shall in nowise be cast out." (2 Nephi 25:26-27, 29.)

The best test of all is the personal test. The Book of Mormon contains a promise that the reader who is truly sincere will receive a manifestation of its truth directly from God. The promise reads: "When ye shall receive these things, I would exhort you that ye would ask God, the Eternal Father, in the name of Christ, if these things are not true; and if ye shall ask with a sincere heart, with real intent, having faith in Christ, he will manifest the truth of it unto you. And by the power of the Holy Ghost ye may know the truth of all things." (Moroni 10:4-5.) Today, millions of people on the face of the earth who have read the book and who have prayed about it have received confirmation of the Spirit that it is true.

The Doctrine and Covenants

Another book of scripture that has been canonized by The Church of Jesus Christ of Latter-day Saints is the Doctrine and Covenants. This is a collection of divine revelations and inspired declarations given for the establishment and regulation of the kingdom of God on the earth in the last days. Although most of the chapters, or sections, are directed to members of The Church of Jesus Christ of Latter-day Saints, the messages, warnings, and exhortations are for the benefit of all mankind and contain an invitation to all people everywhere to hear the voice of the Lord speaking to them for their temporal well-being and their everlasting salvation. The first section declares: "For verily the voice of the Lord is unto all men, and there is none to escape; and there is no eye that shall not see, neither ear that shall not hear, neither heart that shall not be penetrated. . . . The voice of warning shall be unto all people, by the mouths of my disciples, . . . for I the Lord have commanded them." (D&C 1:2, 4.)

The Pearl of Great Price

The introduction to this fourth book of sacred scripture states that "the Pearl of Great Price is a selection of choice materials touching many significant aspects of the faith and doctrine of The Church of Jesus Christ of Latter-day Saints. These items were produced by the Prophet Joseph Smith and were published in the Church periodicals of his day." These documents include the following:

1. *Selections from the Book of Moses.* This is an extract from the Book of Genesis as divinely translated by Joseph Smith. The contents were revealed to him. The writings are interesting for many reasons, but especially to show how much the ancient prophets knew about Jesus Christ, which knowledge had been lost. In this book we see that Adam knew about Jesus and taught baptism; Enoch preached Jesus (other Enoch texts have been uncovered recently, but Joseph Smith wrote this document more than 150 years ago); Methuselah, Noah, and Moses all knew of and taught Jesus Christ by name and concept. This book is an exciting scriptural treasure.

2. *The Book of Abraham.* This is a translation from some Egyptian papyri that came into the hands of Joseph Smith in 1835. The scripture contains some writings by the ancient prophet Abraham concerning our premortal life, the creation, the choosing of a Redeemer, and the placing of Adam and Eve in the Garden of Eden.

3. *Joseph Smith–Matthew.* This is an extract from the translation of the Bible as revealed to Joseph Smith in 1831, including Matthew 23:39 and the twenty-fourth chapter of Matthew. In this extract, Jesus foretells the impending destruction of Jerusalem and discourses on His second coming and the destruction of the wicked.

4. *Joseph Smith–History.* In this short selection, Joseph Smith bears testimony to the events leading to restoration of the Church in this dispensation. He tells of his ancestry and family; his desire to seek wisdom, after having read James 1:5; his first vision, in which the Father and the Son appeared to him and called him to his ministry; the persecution heaped upon him as a result of his testimony; the appearance of an angel named Moroni, who revealed to him gold plates that were subsequently translated into a book now known as the Book of Mormon; and a visitation from John the Baptist with the subsequent baptism of Joseph and his scribe, Oliver Cowdery.

5. *The Articles of Faith.* These are thirteen statements by the Prophet Joseph Smith concerning some basic beliefs of members

of The Church of Jesus Christ of Latter-day Saints. They were included in a letter to the editor of a Chicago newspaper, in which
the Prophet wrote a short history of the Church as well as explained some of the doctrines unique to its members.

Lost Scriptures

In the Bible, many other books of scripture are mentioned. We
believe that one day these scriptures will come forth and that they
will add to the faith of all Christians. They include the "book of
the covenant" mentioned in Exodus 24:7; the book of "wars of the
Lord" in Numbers 21:14; the book of Jasher (Joshua 10:13 and 2
Samuel 1:18); the acts of Solomon (1 Kings 11:41); Nathan the
prophet (2 Chronicles 9:29); Shemaiah (2 Chronicles 12:15); acts
of Abijah (2 Chronicles 13:22); Jehu (2 Chronicles 20:34); and
Paul's epistle from Laodicia (Colossians 4:16). Other "lost" books
of scripture are mentioned in the Book of Mormon: the words of
Zenos (Jacob 1:5); the words of Zenock and of Neum (1 Nephi
13:26); and Ezias (Alma 63:12). In the Doctrine and Covenants
we learn about the book of Enoch (D&C 107:57), and the writings
of Lehi, a portion of the translation of the Book of Mormon that
was lost when Joseph Smith allowed it to pass from his custody (see
introduction to D&C 3).

We believe that other lost civilizations have had Christian
prophets and that they will someday be heard from. In the Book of
Mormon we read: "After it [the Bible] had come forth unto them I
beheld other books, which came forth by the power of the Lamb."
(1 Nephi 13:39.) And finally, we believe that sealed portions of
the Book of Mormon that Joseph Smith was not allowed to translate will someday be opened, and when that time comes, they will
surely contain more information and testimony that Jesus is the
Son of God and the only name through which salvation is available to mankind.

We Believe That Christ Will Return to Reign Personally upon the Earth

When He was upon the earth in the meridian of time, Jesus taught His disciples that "when the Son of man shall come in his glory, and all the holy angels with him, then shall he sit on the throne of his glory." (Matthew 25:31.) Members of The Church of Jesus Christ of Latter-day Saints believe in the Second Coming of Christ in all His glory, that He will reign personally upon the earth, and that the earth will be renewed and will receive its paradisiacal glory. Following the Second Coming, the period known as the Millennium will take place, with the resurrection of all mankind as foretold by Christ and the prophets.

Those who accept Christ as the Redeemer, the Savior, the Lamb who was slain before the foundation of the world, find great significance in His words and teachings with regard to the Second Coming as well as in Old Testament prophecies that refer to this same anticipated event.

Isaiah taught: "Be strong, fear not: behold, your God will come with a vengeance, even God with a recompence; he will come and save you." (Isaiah 35:4.) And again, "Behold, the Lord God will come with strong hand, and his arm shall rule for him: behold, his reward is with him, and his work before him. He shall feed his flock like a shepherd: he shall gather the lambs with his arm, and carry them in his bosom, and shall gently lead those that are with young." (Isaiah 40:10-11.) In the book of Psalms, we find several statements concerning this blessed event, the Second Coming, including these: "Our God shall come, and shall not keep silence"

(50:3); "He shall have dominion also from sea to sea, and from the river unto the ends of the earth" (72:8); "When the Lord shall build up Zion, he shall appear in his glory" (102:16). Malachi declares: "The Lord, whom ye seek, shall suddenly come to his temple" (3:1); "But who may abide the day of his coming?" (3:2); and "I will send you Elijah the prophet before the coming of the great and dreadful day of the Lord" (4:5).

In the Gospels, the Savior and his disciples talked about the Second Coming. We read: "Then shall they see the Son of man coming in the clouds with great power and glory" (Mark 13:26), and "Be ye therefore ready also: for the Son of man cometh at an hour when ye think not" (Luke 12:40). After the Savior's crucifixion and resurrection, leaders of the church that He had established taught concerning His Second Coming. For example, in his first epistle to the Thessalonians, Paul wrote: "The Lord himself shall descend from heaven with a shout, with the voice of the archangel, and with the trump of God" (4:16).

The Book of Mormon prophets looked forward to the Second Coming. Among their teachings are these: "The time cometh speedily that the righteous must be led up as calves of the stall, and the Holy One of Israel must reign in dominion, and might, and power, and great glory" (1 Nephi 22:24); "The bands of death shall be broken, and the Son reigneth, and hath power over the dead; therefore, he bringeth to pass the resurrection of the dead" (Mosiah 15:20); and "Then shall the power of heaven come down among them; and I [Christ] also will be in the midst" (3 Nephi 21:25).

Much has been written about the period just before the Second Coming. At one time Christ's disciples asked Him, "Master, when shall these things be? and what sign will there be when these things shall come to pass?" He replied:

"Many shall come in my name, saying, I am Christ. . . . But when ye shall hear of wars and commotions, be not terrified: for these things must first come to pass; but the end is not by and by.

"Then said he unto them, Nation shall rise against nation, and kingdom against kingdom: and great earthquakes shall be in divers places, and famines, and pestilences; and fearful sights and great signs shall there be from heaven. . . .

"There shall be signs in the sun, and in the moon, and in the stars; and upon the earth distress of nations, with perplexity; the sea and the waves roaring; men's hearts failing them for fear, and for looking after those things which are coming on the earth: for the powers of heaven shall be shaken.

"And then shall they see the Son of man coming in a cloud with power and great glory." (Luke 21:7-11, 25-27.)

A similar revelation was given in modern times through the Prophet Joseph Smith:

"The hour is nigh and the day soon at hand when the earth is ripe; and all the proud and they that do wickedly shall be as stubble; and I will burn them up, saith the Lord of Hosts, that wickedness shall not be upon the earth. . . .

"The sun shall be darkened, and the moon shall be turned into blood, and the stars shall fall from heaven, and there shall be greater signs in heaven above and in the earth beneath; and there shall be weeping and wailing among the hosts of men; and there shall be a great hailstorm sent forth to destroy the crops of the earth.

"And it shall come to pass, because of the wickedness of the world, that I will take vengeance upon the wicked, for they will not repent; for the cup of mine indignation is full; for behold, my blood shall not cleanse them if they hear me not.

"Wherefore, I the Lord God will send forth flies upon the face of the earth, which shall take hold of the inhabitants thereof, and shall eat their flesh, and shall cause maggots to come in upon them." (D&C 29:9, 14-19.)

We do not know exactly when this tragic final period and the Second Coming will take place. But there are a good many things that we can piece out from the scriptures that help us in watching the timetable of God. We know, for example, that the gospel needs to be preached in all nations and in all tongues on the face of the earth, and we know some specifics that need to happen to the Jews and the lost tribes of Israel in order to fulfill ancient prophecies.

It is interesting that some people seem to want to wait as long as possible before they change their lives to live according to that judgment day which is surely coming. For example, I have a friend

who was living a comfortable life overseas with his yacht anchored
in a tropical bay, his condominium in the city, his investments in
the local economy, and other investments back home in the
United States. He heard a fiery sermon on the Second Coming
and began to worry about returning home. His question was,
"Bob, you ought to know. How close is the end of the world? I
don't think I can sell out very easily right now. What is the real
story anyway?" My answer was not in jest—it was serious. I told
him that I thought he had a little time. I said, "If we have to wait
until the gospel is preached in all of India, Africa, and the countries behind the bamboo and iron curtains, it looks like it will be a
while. There is a softening but not yet an open door to preach
Christianity in every language and dialect.

"Besides," I continued, "the last great battle will have to be
fought at Jerusalem, some prophets need to come to preach Christ
to the Jews, a New Jerusalem that will be worthy of the presence of
the Savior needs to be built on the American continent, and so
on. In fact, I think you may have a number of years in which to sell
your investments and move home. But that should not worry you.
You have a much greater risk. At your age and with your health,
what you really need to be doing, my friend, is preparing to meet
the Lord this very night."

Then I told my friend about the rich man who had a great deal
of worldly goods but who had forgotten about death and God:

"The ground of a certain rich man brought forth plentifully;
and he thought within himself, saying, What shall I do, because I
have no room where to bestow my fruits?

"And he said, This will I do: I will pull down my barns, and
build greater; and there will I bestow all my fruits and my goods.
And I will say to my soul, Soul, thou hast much goods laid up for
many years; take thine ease, eat, drink, and be merry.

"But God said unto him, Thou fool, this night thy soul shall be
required of thee: then whose shall those things be, which thou
hast provided? So is he that layeth up treasure for himself, and is
not rich toward God." (Luke 12:16-21.)

I told my friend that he had better be concerned about putting
his life in order so that he would not fear dying at any moment. At
the same time he should not concern himself with how much

55

profit he might make by selling his investments; in fact, perhaps he should keep them. I suggested that his first priority should be how close he was to the Lord and how close he was to his loved ones; how close he was to being the kind of person he knew he should be. My friend did align his perspective with eternal values and set about putting his life in order.

People have long speculated about the end of the earth and the Second Coming. The truth is, however, that "the hour and the day no man knoweth, neither the angels in heaven, nor shall they know until he comes." (D&C 49:7.) Jesus says, "Watch therefore, for ye know neither the day nor the hour wherein the Son of man cometh." (Matthew 25:13.)

The Second Coming will be a magnificent event. Christ will be accompanied by the hosts of righteous people who have already passed from this life to the spirit world beyond. The saintly people alive here on earth are to be quickened and caught up to meet Him and then to descend with Him as partakers of and participants in His glory. The kingdom of heaven under the direction of the Savior himself will be comprised of all nations. Christ will personally rule and reign on the earth, which He has redeemed at the sacrifice of His own life.

Prior to His coming, Israel is to be gathered and an earthly Zion is to be established. The wicked will be destroyed in the closing scenes of what is termed the "old earth." Satan will be bound, and Christ will reign for a period spoken of as the Millennium. The scriptures tell us that some of the dead shall not live again until the thousand years are over, while the righteous will live and reign with Christ. (Revelation 20:4-5.)

Isaiah tells us that the Savior will "create new heavens and a new earth. . . . There shall be no more thence an infant of days, nor an old man that hath not filled his days. . . . The wolf and the lamb shall feed together, and the lion shall eat straw like the bullock." (Isaiah 65:17, 20, 25.)

Other scriptures in the Bible that describe the Millennium include these:

"Thus saith the Lord God; In the day that I shall have cleansed you from all your iniquities I will also cause you to dwell in the cities, and the wastes shall be builded. And the desolate land shall be tilled, whereas it lay desolate in the sight of all that passed by. And they shall say, This land that was desolate is become like the garden of Eden; and the waste and desolate and ruined cities are become fenced, and are inhabited." (Ezekiel 36:33-35.)

"We, according to his promise, look for new heavens and a new earth, wherein dwelleth righteousness. Wherefore, beloved, seeing that ye look for such things, be diligent that ye may be found of him in peace, without spot, and blameless." (2 Peter 3:13-14.)

In the Book of Mormon we are told that "all things which have been revealed unto the children of men shall at that day be revealed; and Satan shall have power over the hearts of the children of men no more, for a long time." (2 Nephi 30:18.)

Yes, we are Christians because we believe in the reality of the Second Coming of Christ and the Millennium of peace that will follow. We believe "all that God has revealed, all that He does now reveal, and we believe that He will yet reveal many great and important things" pertaining to that glorious time. (See Article of Faith 9.) We urge all people everywhere to prepare themselves now through righteous living and obedience to the commandments of God so that they may be partakers of these great blessings to come.

We Are Christians Because . . .

We Believe in Spiritual Gifts
as in the Primitive Church

The seventh Article of Faith of the Church states that "we believe in the gift of tongues, prophecy, revelation, visions, healing, interpretation of tongues, and so forth." These are spiritual gifts that existed in the church of Christ when it was on the earth in the meridian of time and that exist in His church today.

Whenever the authority to act in the name of God has been on the earth in the form of a legally authorized priesthood operating within the framework of His church, the members have been blessed in their faith through spiritual gifts. Such gifts can appropriately be regarded as one of the essential characteristics of the true church. The days of miracles have not been replaced by modern sophistry except in the lives of those who do not have faith to see. Spiritual gifts are not given to impress or to convert. They are given only for the benefit and strengthening of those who already have the faith to believe. Spiritual gifts and what we call miracles are given to those who love the Lord and who live His commandments.

We believe in all the miracles of the scriptures, including the parting of the Red Sea, the miracles that Moses performed for the Pharaoh's benefit, the day the sun stopped, the trumpets of Joshua causing the walls of Jericho to fall down, David's triumph over Goliath, Daniel in the lion's den, and others in Old Testament times as well as all of the miracles Jesus performed.

We try to be reverent about sacred experiences and to avoid sharing them with those who do not understand and respect matters of the spirit. However, hardly a member of The Church of Jesus Christ of Latter-day Saints has not experienced a miracle that has edified the person's faith and shown that the Lord can and does do great miracles in this modern age of space shuttles and satellites, just as He did in biblical times. The restoration of the Church in this dispensation has brought to pass many visions, prophecies, and revelations, and these are formally recorded for the benefit of those who are interested. If one is in tune with the Spirit, the Lord will bear witness that these things are true and that the Church was restored through the power of God.

The gifts of tongues and interpretation of tongues have both ancient and modern applications. They are gifts of the Spirit that allow communication despite language barriers. On the Day of Pentecost, some thought the brethren were drunk, until they began to hear the gospel in their own tongues; then they wanted to be baptized. In pioneer days, experiences were recorded in which a person would talk in a language he or she did not understand and then another person would interpret for the congregation the spiritual message that had been given. Through the Spirit, those who listened would have a reconfirmation that the interpretation was correct and that the message was for their benefit and had come from the Lord.

In my own life I have been blessed with a facility with language that to me is one form of the gift of tongues because it surpasses what I think should be possible through normal study and usage. There were times during my first two years in South America as a young missionary when I knew that sometimes I was able to understand more than I had any right to understand and spoke with greater vocabulary and fluidity than I had any reason to expect. These occasions came only when I was teaching an interested investigator of the Church or when I was preaching from a pulpit. I have seen missionaries struggle and study for months and finally arrive at that moment of spiritual breakthrough that to them is the gift of tongues, when they could suddenly speak and understand the language. On other occasions I have seen missionaries in Latin America who have made such a poor presentation of their message that I could not tell what they were saying in either English or Spanish, and yet the responsive investigator understood by the

Spirit or through the interpretation of tongues. One new missionary in Mexico, fascinated by this phenomenon, exclaimed to me, "This is great! It's as if my spirit steps out of me, and the investigator's spirit steps out of him, and my spirit teaches his spirit while I struggle with my Spanish."

Another of the gifts that we believe in is the gift of prophecy. We do not believe that the spirit of prophecy is limited to those who preside in the Church. We sustain the members of the First Presidency and the Quorum of the Twelve Apostles as prophets, seers, and revelators to the Church, but we also believe that each of us may from time to time enjoy the spirit of prophecy. An early member of the Church wrote in his journal that the Saints had met in a wooded area where each took turns, going around the circle, "to exercise our gift of prophecy."

When I was a young missionary in South America, my companion and I traveled across the Andes Mountains from Argentina into Chile. The Church had been in Argentina for twenty-five years with very little growth, and there were no Latter-day Saints in Chile at the time. In fact, we were the first missionaries in Chile since Elder Parley P. Pratt had preached there one hundred years earlier. We were extremely impressed with the spirituality of the people, and I felt very strongly that the day would come when all of Latin America would have many members of the Church, when there would be many Latter-day Saint chapels, and even when temples would dot the land. Today I marvel that in just over thirty years, the Church has grown from a few thousand members in Latin America to more than one million Spanish-speaking and Portuguese-speaking members; from one stake in the Mexican colonies to more than 250 stakes in Mexico, Central America, and South America; from four missions to more than forty missions; from no temples to seven temples. I had a glimpse of the future that led me to cast my lot with Latin America in choosing a career in banking there.

Another aspect of prophecy is frequently found in patriarchal blessings. In my own blessing, the patriarch, speaking directly to me for the Lord, said that my voice would be heard among the nations of the world. I believe that he was prophesying for my benefit. When my parents and my wife's parents asked why we would even consider returning to South America to pursue a career, I showed them my patriarchal blessing and said I felt there was much more for me to do there. They were touched by the same spirit and agreed with me.

I have never had what I would call a vision, yet I believe in visions, and I believe that should the Lord need to instruct me in that manner, I would indeed see a vision. I believe that Joseph Smith had a vision—in fact, that he had many visions. They were all necessary for the restoration of the Church and for the instruction of Joseph himself as the restoring prophet. I believe that all of our prophets have seen visions but that it is not necessary for them to share their experiences with us except when they are instructed to do so.

Healings, another gift of the spirit, are a part of our theology and our spiritual life, just as they were a part of the early Christian church. One of my first recollections was of an accident I suffered when I was a small child. My father had left on a mission to the Southern States the day before the accident, leaving my mother and me on our farm. Mother was heating water on a wood-burning stove and then carrying it to the washing machine. I was playing on the floor, and somehow I ran in front of her and tripped her. The full kettle of boiling water cascaded over my body. We lived sixty miles from the closest doctor or hospital. A hired hand, who was an elder in the Church, ran to a neighboring farm and brought back another member who also held the Melchizedek Priesthood. Together they prepared to anoint me and bless me. My mother, with the faith of an Eve or a Mary, told them, "Heal this boy so his father will not have to come home from his mission." They did so, and added a blessing that not even scars would remain. I remember feeling no pain after the blessing, and when the skin peeled off, there were no complications and no scars. My father continued to serve his mission, and he was not told about my accident until several weeks later, when Mother could tell him that I was all right.

We believe that the Lord has revealed great knowledge to medical science for our benefit and that we should use all that the medical profession has to offer. But we also rely upon our faith, prayers, and the power of the priesthood through anointing and sealing. We follow the counsel of James, who said: "Is any sick among you? let him call for the elders of the church; and let them pray over him, anointing him with oil in the name of the Lord." (James 5:14.)

I once asked a young man who had been called to serve as a bishop in the Church only two years after his conversion how he had come to join the Church. He told me about a Latter-day Saint neighbor family who had tried to interest his family in the gospel. "They did everything," he said. "They brought us magazines and tracts and books, gifts of food, and other things. Then we agreed to let the missionaries come and tell us about the Restoration—but at the end of their message we asked them not to return. However, our neighbors never gave up. They kept inviting us and loving us. Then one day our son became critically ill. We tried first one doctor, then another, then a third, and none could help us. With our little boy in a coma, we returned home, sobbing all the way. Our neighbors saw us coming and asked what had happened. When we told them, the wife said, 'Do you remember those missionaries who came to your home?' I said I did. 'Well, do you remember anything special about them?' I replied that they were very nice and seemed very spiritual. She continued, 'Those missionaries have the power of God to heal the sick in the household of faith. Do you believe they could ask the Lord to heal your little boy?'"

The bishop's eyes misted as he explained to me, "I suppose my faith was partly in desperation, but at that moment it did seem to me that those two missionaries who had taught us about the angel's visit to Joseph Smith were like angels themselves. I believed then that they could ask the Lord for this blessing and that He would hear them and would heal my son. The neighbor told me that the two missionaries were no longer in that area, but that two others had replaced them. She called them, and they came quickly. They anointed our baby, and in a short time he started to recover. Within a few days his health had returned."

We know that God loves all of his children and responds to their prayers and pleas for mercy. Parents may pray for their children, and a loving Heavenly Father, seeing their faith and their tears, will in His wisdom grant blessings. The scriptural process of having the elders anoint and bless can also bring down the powers of heaven. Even so, not every anointing and blessing is met with total or immediate recovery. The Lord has His own purposes, and all we can do is perform the sacred ordinance of anointing and blessing in the prescribed way, exercising all our faith, and then trust in Him to do whatever is best in the long run for us and for those we love. This is the Christlike faith. The literal reality of the ancient gifts of the spirit is a necessary part of modern Christianity.

We Are Christians Because . . .

We Believe in the Eternal Nature of the Family

To Moses on Mount Sinai, the Lord declared: "Honour thy father and thy mother: that thy days may be long upon the land which the Lord thy God giveth thee." (Exodus 20:12.) To another great prophet, Elijah, the keys have been given "of turning the hearts of the fathers to the children, and the hearts of the children to the fathers." (D&C 27:9; Malachi 4:6.)

We are Christians because we follow these commandments; we honor our fathers and our mothers, and our grandparents, and our great-grandparents, and all generations before them. We seek to turn the hearts of the children to their parents and their forefathers, and to turn the hearts of the parents to the children. We strive to protect the integrity of each home and family from the influences of Satan. We have a number of Christ-centered programs that reinforce the roles of the father and mother, and that strengthen the home, the family, and each individual member of the family. We oppose anything that might weaken or destroy the authority of the father and mother in their own family. We believe, as one of our modern prophets taught, that "no other success in life can compensate for failure in the home."

Nearly everything we do in the Church is designed to strengthen the home and the family. The basic unit of the Church is the family. In our Sunday meetings, the young men and their fathers are taught to take their place as spiritual leaders in their homes, while the young women and their mothers learn their responsibilities in contributing to the spirituality, beauty, and order in the home.

As head of his family, each Latter-day Saint father may lead his family in much the same way as a Christian minister leads his flock. He is encouraged to call his family together each day for family prayer; to study the scriptures with them; to call on a family member at each meal to offer a blessing upon the food; to see that the family meets together regularly for family home evening; to teach his family by precept and example the commandments of God. He may give a father's blessing to a family member who is in need of one, such as when an important decision or situation must be faced, or when the child is leaving home for an extended period and needs extra support and encouragement. He may give blessings to family members when they are ill or having medical problems. He may hold regular interviews with his children to encourage them in meeting their goals, to review their daily progress, and to find out how they feel about themselves and their lives. He is truly a patriarch in his home, giving spiritual and practical guidance to each member.

The Latter-day Saint mother is honored by her husband as his partner, his principal counselor in matters that affect their family. She contributes to the beauty, peace, orderliness, cleanliness, and culture in the home. Since she usually spends more time with the children than does her husband, she has great influence on their growth and development. She is usually involved in charitable service to neighbors and brothers and sisters in the gospel. She is expected to develop her own talents and interests through study and practice. She shares with her husband the responsibility for teaching gospel principles and practices to her children. Though the Latter-day Saint mother is expected, if possible, to be available in the home especially when her children are small, all LDS women are encouraged to develop skills and to prepare themselves as much as possible so that they might be self-supporting should the need arise, as well as so that they can better guide and train their children.

Latter-day Saint children are to be taught to respect and obey and honor their parents, just as parents are expected to love their children. The programs of the Church are all established to help both parents and children achieve greater success in their lives and in their homes. With the many forces in the world that teach lessons contrary to Christian principles and do everything they can to entice youth away from the home and its wholesome influence, there are inevitably some young people who do stray. Many parents may not be as well trained in psychology or communication as they need to be in order to combat these outside influences. Sometimes the young person's urge toward independence and self-determination conflicts with the parent's desire to continue to influence the child's actions. The Church, through its programs for young men and young women as well for adults, can help both parents and children learn to understand each other better while guiding them to a personal relationship with their Heavenly Father.

Elijah's mission, the Latter-day Saints believe, is to turn the hearts of the fathers to the children, and the hearts of the children to the fathers. This includes the important work of linking families together through the generations, so that the family unit will continue into eternity. Thus, members of the Church seek information concerning their forefathers and foremothers as far back as possible. This responsibility, the gathering of information about prior generations, explains the emphasis members of the Church place on genealogical research. We believe that it would be tragic for some members of a family to be separated in the Resurrection from other members of the same immediate family. Would we receive all the blessings of heaven if parents were separated from their children, or if grandparents were separated from their grandchildren?

One of the primary reasons Latter-day Saints seek out their progenitors is so that the necessary ordinances can be performed in behalf of those ancestors to continue the family relationship and keep it unbroken. In ancient, or traditional, Christianity, as in Christianity as practiced by the Latter-day Saints, prophets have taught that baptism is essential for those who enter Christ's kingdom. Paul and other disciples of the Savior in the meridian of time knew this—and they taught the importance of baptism for everyone, including those who have gone before. "Else what shall they do which are baptized for the dead, if the dead rise not at all?" Paul asked the Corinthians. "Why are they then baptized?" (1 Corinthians 15:29.)

An entire chapter in this epistle of Paul is devoted to a discussion of death and resurrection. Doesn't it make sense that if a person has never had an oportunity to hear the gospel during his mortal life, he should have that opportunity to be baptized so he can enter the kingdom of God? Thus, the Latter-day Saints practice baptism by proxy, a vicarious ordinance performed for and in behalf of their progenitors. Yes, salvation is a family affair, and our departed loved ones will not be saved without us. We all need each other, "God having provided some better thing for us, that they without us should not be made perfect." (Hebrews 11:40.)

In our own day, the Lord has said through revelation, "Let me assure you that these are principles in relation to the dead and the living that cannot be lightly passed over, as pertaining to our salvation. For their salvation [that is, the salvation of the dead] is necessary and essential to our salvation, as Paul says concerning the fathers—that they without us cannot be made perfect—neither can we without our dead be made perfect. . . .

"It is sufficient to know . . . that the earth will be smitten with a curse unless there is a welding link of some kind or other between the fathers and the children." (D&C 128:15, 18.)

As Christians, Latter-day Saints have a vital interest in their roots, in their genealogy. We want to know the past generations, and we want to have the saving ordinances performed for them. We have built temples, sacred buildings where ordinances in behalf of ourselves and vicarious ordinances for the dead may be performed; in fact, the only place we do the saving ordinances for the dead is in the temple. There we go to perform the ordinances of baptism for the dead and of sealing families together, welding the links between the generations. Our hearts have turned to our fathers!

We Are Christians Because . . .

We Believe in Keeping the Sabbath Day Holy

When the world was created, according to the account in Genesis, "on the seventh day God ended his work which he had made; and he rested. . . . And God blessed the seventh day, and sanctified it." (Genesis 2:2-3.) The importance of this day was underscored when the Ten Commandments were revealed to Moses on Mount Sinai: "Remember the sabbath day, to keep it holy. Six days shalt thou labour, and do all thy work: But the seventh day is the sabbath of the Lord thy God: in it thou shalt not do any work. . . . Wherefore the Lord blessed the sabbath day, and hallowed it." (Exodus 20:8-12.)

Since the beginning of time, one day in seven has been set aside as a day in which we should rest from our labors and worship our Heavenly Father. This is both a blessing for our benefit and a commandment to be obeyed. Many in the Christian world readily accept the idea of resting from their labors, but probably no commandment is abused more frequently by Christians than the one about keeping the Sabbath day holy and worshiping the Lord. Some persons would justify their desecration of the Lord's day by saying that they feel close to God in the mountains or on the lakes. Others simply ignore the commandment to rest from their labors, and continue with their commercial enterprises as if the Lord had never given this commandment.

We feel strongly that a true Christian faithfully observes one day in seven to both rest and worship. Some activities that might be appropriate on the Sabbath day are:

1. Attend organized church services.

2. Have family activities in the home, under the direction of the head of the family, commensurate with the Sabbath, such as individual and family reading of the scriptures, singing of hymns, discussion of spiritual subjects, review of principles learned at church, and a personal interview between parent and child on goals, plans, conduct, and obedience, all in a loving and caring atmosphere.

3. Visit the sick and homebound, the elderly, loved ones, and friends.

4. Carry out necessary church assignments, such as attending choir rehearsal, attending ecclesiastical interviews, preparing church reports, and attending to church administrative matters.

5. Read uplifting material in books and magazines that are appropriate for a good Christian home.

6. Write letters to friends and loved ones.

7. Write in a personal or family journal or history.

8. Work on family photograph books and collect family souvenirs.

9. Work on genealogy.

10. Call friends and family members on the telephone.

Among activities that might be considered inappropriate on the Sabbath are attendance at sports events, theaters, movies, and other public entertainment, shopping, and participating in sports or any other activity that would detract from the sacred nature of the day.

Some may ask whether any work is appropriate for the Sabbath. The Savior indicated that if the ox is in the mire, one is justified in getting him out, even though it is the Sabbath. Some work on the Lord's day may be necessary at times and in reasonable emergencies. A farmer has to feed the stock, milk the cows, and so forth. A policeman, fireman, doctor, bus driver, or other employee may find that his profession requires working at times on the Sabbath in order to handle some basic functions of our society. Sometimes people find themselves obliged, in order to earn a living and support a family, to take employment that requires work on the Sabbath, while refusal to comply might create a more severe hardship on the dependents. This we do not judge; we only ask that each person be guided by his or her own conscience. If there is flexibility in the work schedule, perhaps the person can trade off with another employee so that work on the Sabbath is not necessary.

Some entrepreneurs justify remaining open on the Sabbath by saying that they must compete with other businesses that have opted to be open for business on the Lord's day. We encourage all business owners and managers to observe the Sabbath and to let their employees observe the Sabbath also. We also believe in supporting businesses that do close on the Sabbath, while at the same time we recognize that some essential services are needed on that day. In addition, we support lawmakers who recommend ordinances and laws that help make our communities more Sabbath oriented. However, we also teach that each individual has the right to make his own choices. We teach Christian principles, but we believe that each person should be able to govern himself.

In a modern revelation, given through the Prophet Joseph Smith, Latter-day Saints are commanded concerning their obligations toward the Sabbath:

"And that thou mayest more fully keep thyself unspotted from the world, thou shalt go to the house of prayer and offer up thy sacraments upon my holy day; for verily this is a day appointed unto you to rest from your labors, and to pay thy devotions unto the Most High;

"Nevertheless thy vows shall be offered up in righteousness on all days and at all times; but remember that on this, the Lord's day, thou shalt offer thine oblations and thy sacraments unto the Most High, confessing thy sins unto thy brethren, and before the Lord.

"And on this day thou shalt do none other thing, only let thy food be prepared with singleness of heart that thy fasting may be perfect, or, in other words, that thy joy may be full."

Those who keep this commandment are then given these great promises:

"Inasmuch as ye do these things with thanksgiving, with cheerful hearts and countenances, . . . the fulness of the earth is yours. . . . He who doeth the works of righteousness shall receive his reward, even peace in this world, and eternal life in the world to come." (D&C 59:15-16, 23.)

We Are Christians Because . . .

We Believe in Being Honest
with the Lord and Our Fellowman

One of the Ten Commandments states: "Thou shalt not steal." (Exodus 20:15.) As Latter-day Saints, we believe that a true Christian is honest in all his dealings with both his fellowman and the Lord. We interpret this commandment in its strictest sense: one should not steal from his neighbor, his employer, the government, or from anyone, under any circumstances.

In Malachi we read: "Will a man rob God? Yet ye have robbed me. But ye say, Wherein have we robbed thee? In tithes and offerings." (Malachi 3:8.) Failure to render to God our tithes and offerings is to rob Him of that which is rightfully His. We testify that millions of Latter-day Saints believe and practice this ancient principle and find that because of their faithfulness and obedience, they are blessed. They render unto the Lord ten percent of their increase and find that the Lord returns to them great blessings, for he has said, "Prove me now herewith . . . if I will not open you the windows of heaven, and pour you out a blessing, that there shall not be room enough to receive it." (Malachi 3:10.) We believe that it is much better to live on ninety percent of our income and the blessings of the Lord than to try to make it safely through the risks of this uncertain world on our own wisdom alone.

The Christian ethic of personal honesty, integrity, and trustworthiness is much needed in today's world of sagging morals. We believe that it is greater to be trusted than to be loved; the world is in great need of people who can be fully trusted and who can withstand temptation. We have no hesitation in saying that a person who is well-grounded in Christian values and character can keep himself unstained from bribery, theft, rationalization, and conflict of interest in which his judgment might be compromised. Just as Joseph of Egypt could not be seduced by Potiphar's wife, so there are many good Christians today who cannot be seduced by offers of goods, services, favors, or anything else that is offered in return for favored position or bribery.

We also believe in paying our honest share toward having a free government. We believe in honestly paying our taxes and other obligations; to do otherwise would be a kind of theft. We encourage honesty in government, efficient and correct administration, reduction of wasteful practices, and in honoring and sustaining the law. One of our basic tenets is: "We believe in being subject to kings, presidents, rulers, and magistrates, in obeying, honoring, and sustaining the law." (Article of Faith 12.) Thus, Latter-day Saints support the government and its leaders in every country in which they live.

Lack of honesty in the workplace is one of the greatest problems of industry and business today. The so-called "insider" theft is one of modern management's biggest concerns, and the costs are greater than those incurred through robbery, burglary, and other larcenous crimes. We believe that the Christian should be honest in all his dealings. Thus, we deplore any stealing or dishonesty from employers, whether it be pilfering of supplies, misuse and stealing of time, or such "white-collar" crimes as falsifying records, gaining access to classified computer information, or juggling records of inventory. All should be labeled as stealing.

In today's society, basic honesty as taught by Christianity is so lacking that some have labeled dishonesty or cheating an epidemic, a hemorrhage of values. It happens in school examinations. It happens in welfare programs, sometimes even into the second and third generation, as recipients of welfare assistance receive payments from two or more agencies at once, or from both state and church, without reporting the dual payments. Some use false identities to obtain excess benefits.

Dishonesty is found in the rampant use of credit-card numbers to make telephone calls. It is found in institutions and businesses, where, according to one report, as many as fifty percent of the employees use postage meters for their personal mail. It happens in various kinds of competition. It happens in commercial establishments, where pilferage by employees and shoplifting by customers lead to the need for higher markups for merchandise and for security systems to be installed. It happens in research, where results are falsified in order to achieve prestige and acclaim when none is due. Cheating happens in marriages. Cheating happens even in diets, the ultimate absurdity. Our world truly needs a return to basic Christian standards of honesty!

One father said to me recently, "I need help. When I was young, I seemed to know the difference between right and wrong. But this new generation can't seem to tell the difference as easily. My son has no standard to guide him in decisions. Where did I go wrong? Or is it the fault of the world we live in?"

My response was that it is partly the fault of the wickedness around us, but parents must also share some of the blame. It is still their responsibility to teach Christian standards in such a way that the next generation will have a higher standard than our own, or will at least have more success than we have had. Church leaders and church programs can help set such high ethics and standards and support the parents in teaching and inspiring youth, but the ultimate responsibility is still that of parents.

Another form of dishonesty, one that is generally more hidden and more insidious than direct theft, is a situation in which one allows his judgment to be impaired by bribes or favors in conflict with the interests of his employer. Sometimes executives entrusted by their supervisors to make key decisions between two or more competitors for important contracts will fall prey to conflict of interest. For example, a loan officer at a bank was the key man on the credit committee that approved large loans for clients. During a period of tight money, he had to decide which of the clients to take care of and which to turn down, since funds were not available for all. One of the clients found a weakness in the loan officer; he found that the man liked expensive fishing trips, so air fare, a chartered boat, and other accommodations were provided. The credit officer's justification was that it didn't hurt the bank in any way for him to choose to give the loan to his "friends." However, when his indiscretion became known to his superiors, he was immediately fired. Once a person has a character flaw, temptations allow his judgment to become even more impaired.

Sometimes an employee will accept a kickback, which can impair his judgment and stand in the way of his working for the best interests of his employer. For instance, an executive is given the assignment to locate a new plant site in a certain area. He finds out the local prices and knows the going values. Then a real bargain unexpectedly appears that is far below market value. The seller is so much in need of the sale that he offers the agent a chance to pocket a kickback commission and still get the property for his company at less than appraised value. Should such a person cave in to Satan's temptation, he will never be worthy of the trust of his superiors—or of the Lord, who knows all things. The day of judgment will come. The only source of true peace in our lives is to live the commandments in such a way that we have nothing to hide— not in this life nor in the day of judgment to come.

At the beginning of this chapter, we discussed briefly the importance of dealing honestly with the Lord. Sometimes people will rationalize their failure to contribute to the church of their choice by saying that they do not know or approve of what is to be done with the funds. The Lord did not say "Bring your tithes to my church *if* you approve of how they are to be used." He said, "Bring ye all the tithes into the storehouse, that there may be meat in mine house."

In The Church of Jesus Christ of Latter-day Saints, no tithing funds are used to pay ecclesiastical leaders. The contributions all go toward building up the kingdom of God. But even in other churches that do not have tithing, I have friends who do tithe and who are abundantly blessed by the Lord for their understanding of and faithfulness to this principle. The wonder is that more churches do not function on this basis and that so few Christians practice it fully.

Faithful tithe payers learn that the Lord will bless those who recognize that "the earth is the Lord's, and the fulness thereof," and that any material blessings we have, even our very health, come from Him.

For example, I was once accompanying a mission president on

a tour of his mission. As we entered one chapel a man approached us with a frown on his face and said to the mission president, "You made a mistake." When the mission president looked puzzled, the man went on, "I mean you made a mistake in not asking for part of the increased income I would have after I paid my tithing." Then they laughed and embraced each other as they told me of their arrangement. The local brother had told the mission president that he did not have enough income from his small business to pay his tithing. The president then promised the man that if he would pay a full and honest tithing, he would have increased blessings and faith. The man now testified that his business had increased substantially after he began paying his tithing, and he also had greater wisdom to manage his affairs.

Another sister testified how, after she paid her tithing fully, she figured out how to sew sleeves on clothing faster at the factory where she worked, and since she was paid by the piece, her income increased. In fact, she was soon asked to help train others and given a higher, fixed salary.

My family, when living on the farm, once had a serious financial dilemma. When we finished the harvest and calculated the year's income, we found that the tithing due the Lord was about the same amount as that which was due the bank for the mortgage; there was only enough money to pay one or the other. After a family council, it was decided that we would pay the tithing to the Lord and then rely on His inspiration or His mercy to soften the banker's heart. The day after the check for tithing in full was given to the bishop, a canning company representative appeared at the farm to contract in advance for the next year's harvest. The amount of the advance payment was enough to meet the mortgage payment at the bank.

Such stories could be told by many faithful tithe payers. It is a true principle—the Lord will bless those who are honest with Him. Our gratitude is little enough as it is, even when we give Him His ten percent. We suppose that He could inspire the prophet and head of the Church with knowledge of where gold lies buried or where to buy oil leases, but that is not the way He works. If He did, we would not be blessed nor would we develop our own faith and trust in Him. When we pay an honest tithe, He will bless us, and we will see His blessings clearly. Never have I known a full tithe payer who felt that the Lord owed him something for his honesty and for not stealing from God. It never works that way. We are always in debt to Him because He opens the windows of heaven upon us and blesses us abundantly.

We Are Christians Because . . .

We Believe in Bearing
True Witness in All Things

Latter-day Saints strive always to obey the Judeo-Christian commandment, "Thou shalt not bear false witness." (Exodus 20:16.) To this, we add that we bear a *true* witness that Jesus is the Christ, that He died on the cross for our sins, that He was resurrected the third day, that He lives, and that He stands personally at the head of the church that bears His name today. We testify as true witnesses that His gospel in its fullness has been restored to the earth. We want to share this truth with everyone; thus, missionary work is a Christian tradition of which we are happy to be part.

If any society is to function properly and avoid chaos, each person bears responsibility for always telling the truth. Even the most primitive societies and cultures have ways to correct and chastize an errant member whose word cannot be trusted. There is always a chance that one witness might be innocently mistaken or that one witness would have a grudge or bias that might lead him to give false witness, so the scriptures speak of the need for two witnesses to establish for certain any point at issue. As a point of law, two or more witnesses are usually sufficient to convict or free a person, depending upon the question at hand.

In past times, even up to the last generation in most so-called Christian countries, a man's word was his bond, and written contracts were seldom needed. Today, however, even in the most thoroughly Christian countries, little of a business or commercial nature can be relied upon by word only.

A simple illustration of a practical application of the need to never bear false witness is found in the following example. A young man advanced in the bank for which he worked until he became head of the current-accounts section. There, he was responsible for thousands of checking-account records of the bank's clients. It was his duty to make certain that all the daily transactions involved in deposits to and withdrawals from the accounts were balanced each night.

Several days after the man took charge of the section, a discrepancy in the accounts appeared. He felt embarrassed that an error should appear so soon after his promotion, but rather than report it, he decided to work that night until he found the error. An error found overnight could easily be corrected the next day, he decided, so he signed the report form saying that all was balanced. Then he worked all night—but didn't find the error. The next day he continued to search the records, and when he couldn't find it, he worked along all the next night, still trying to spot the flaw but to no avail. The third day, quite by coincidence, a client asked for a report on his account balance, and upon finding an error, he reported it to management.

For the first time the bank managers became aware that the current-accounts records had, for two days, been unbalanced, though the new section head had reported that they were balanced. The bonding company required that any employee who knowingly-falsified a report to cover an error must be terminated, since this indicated a character flaw that would sooner or later lead to a second occurrence. The young man lost his job as a result.

In all organized business, the rule is—and must be—"Never sign anything that is not true to the best of your knowledge, no matter what the consequence." In other words, never bear false witness. This rule applies in every other situation of life, be it a test at school, a sworn document for a matter at law, a tax matter, an accounting or inventory statement, a social conversation, or anything else.

But rather than dwell on the negative aspects of this rule, let us turn to the positive. Let us always remember our Christian responsibility to bear a true witness of spiritual things we know to be true. I find it very interesting to note that when the Savior was crucified, it was not for His miracles or doctrines. What most in-furiated the Jews was the calm testimony, the witness, He bore that He was the Son of God. He was crucified for blasphemy, for being so bold as to bear a true witness.

The same thing happened to Paul. He related, as a true wit-ness, the spiritual experience he had had on the way to Damascus and how he saw a light and heard a voice. But his true witness caused his listeners to mock him and persecute him.

When Stephen bore witness of his vision of "the glory of God, and Jesus standing on the right hand of God," the people "stopped their ears" and stoned him to death. (Acts 7:55-60.) They did not want to hear more of his testimony or true witness.

It is also interesting to note that when the Savior was resur-rected, He did not appear to His tormentors and say, "See, you couldn't stop me. You killed me, but here I am again." Nor did He appear in the midst of the Sanhedrin to cause consternation and fear. He appeared only to those of His close associates who already believed in Him, and He told them to go and bear witness that they had seen the resurrected Christ. A true witness is all that is re-quired, and the Holy Ghost will tell the listener, if that person is prepared to hear, that the witness is really true.

The primary reason we Latter-day Saints do missionary work is to bear heartfelt witness of the blessings we have received, of the impressions we have felt in our hearts, of the knowledge we have been given that we know to be true, of our prayers that have been answered, of the times we have been lifted up far above our normal selves, of the situations in which we have been privileged to be in-struments in the hands of the Lord, of the burning we have felt in our bosom when we have read a certain scripture or heard a certain sermon preached, of what we have felt when we have participated in a sacred ordinance. Then the Spirit can testify to the listener that what he has just heard is true, that the person who bears tes-timony is a true servant with a message that he should listen to, that the Church to which the testifier belongs is the true church of Jesus Christ upon the earth, with the legal authority to act in His name.

Our missionary message can be summed up in these three pur-poses: to testify of—

1. The divine Sonship of Jesus Christ,

2. The divine mission of Joseph Smith as a witness to the Father and the Son as well as to bring forth the Book of Mormon, another witness to Jesus Christ, and

3. The divine nature of the Church of Jesus Christ.

We go forth to our own nation as well as other nations of the earth with that simple witness because we have been commanded to do so. We go to Christian nations as well as non-Christian nations to testify that we have additional knowledge of Christ that is valuable to every person who professes to follow the Savior.

We Are Christians Because . . .

We Believe in the Highest Standards of Virtue and Morality

When He gave the Ten Commandments to the Israelites, the Lord declared: "Thou shalt not commit adultery." In the Sermon on the Mount, Jesus gave the higher law: "Ye have heard that it was said by them of old time, Thou shalt not commit adultery: but I say unto you, That whosoever looketh on a woman to lust after her hath committed adultery with her already in his heart." (Matthew 5:28.) *

It is clear from the scriptures that adultery is, in the mind of God and of the prophets, one of the greatest sins and evils, second only to murder. In the time of Moses, and even down to the time of the Savior, it was punishable by death, usually stoning in a public place. Though those harsh penalties are no longer imposed or practiced by church or state, the seriousness of the sin has not changed.

We live in an age when there is a great deal of promiscuity, with a deterioration of standards of dress, language, and conduct, and that should only cause all Christians to rally to the cause of the Savior. Just because so many people have given in to Satan does not mean that the standards have changed in the eyes of the Lord. We disagree with the so-called modern morality and situational ethics preached by many self-appointed philosophers, who say, in essence, "Do what you want. Don't feel guilty. There's no such

---

*Though the scriptures use the masculine gender, we believe that Christ was warning both men and women against moral transgressions.

thing as sin." We declare that God has revealed absolutes to His people that do not change with time or circumstances. As a church, we follow the teachings of the Savior and the prophets that we must control our thoughts, avoid immorality and indecency in all forms, totally avoid the sins of fornication and adultery, and strive to keep ourselves virtuous and pure in all respects.

We live in an age when youth as well as adults are bombarded on all sides by worldly influences that are contrary to the teachings of the Savior. Song lyrics are often sexually explicit, television and movie scripts make sex outside of marriage seem glamorous and acceptable, many magazine articles discuss illicit subjects openly, peers exaggerate their own sins rather than taking pride in chastity, and virtue is made to appear old-fashioned and even unattractive. We believe that every parent has a responsibility to teach his children how to distinguish right from wrong—and to choose the right in all things. "Train up a child in the way he should go," the Old Testament declares, "and when he is old, he will not depart from it." (Proverbs 22:6.)

The programs of The Church of Jesus Christ of Latter-day Saints are designed to help parents in their task of strengthening the youth, providing positive peer-group support for virtue, cleanliness, morality, modesty, and chastity. Clean, wholesome activities are provided, and lessons have been written to reinforce the importance of being morally clean.

In pioneer days, every member of the family, young and old alike, was involved in helping to support the family. Long hours of arduous work were involved, and young people were usually so exhausted at the end of the day that they were ready to rest and sleep. "An idle brain is the devil's workshop," says an English proverb. Today, with so many time- and labor-saving devices available to most families, more time is available to pursue personal interests. Wise parents will see that their children's days and evenings are filled with study, sports activities, hobbies, part-time jobs, family projects, music or other lessons, and other activities that will direct their minds in positive ways. Parents and church leaders will help build self-confidence in youth so they will not need approval from adverse peer pressure. They will help young people to have a farsighted, even eternal, perspective rather than a shortsighted, here-and-now philosophy. They will help them to develop a positive approach to life without falling victim to the enticements of Satan and his associates.

Parents whose home is Christ-centered will help young people realize that many movies, television programs, novels, and magazines exaggerate the romantic emphasis on sex in order to sell the sensational, and that real life can and should be different. In a Christ-centered home, young people will learn that the intimate relationship between parents, bound together in the holy bond of matrimony, is wholesome and right in the sight of the Lord. They will learn that beliefs and goals should be set within the framework of religion and the teachings of the Church.

In the Church of Christ, parents and youth can develop their unique gifts and talents and establish good Christian relationships that will help build within each person a positive self-image. As praise and recognition are given, everyone can feel accepted, loved, and recognized as a person of great worth.

The Church reinforces the teachings of parents concerning modesty in dress, the importance of not dating before age sixteen, and proper conduct when a youth is with a member of the opposite sex. Our prophets speak forthrightly on these subjects, and their counsel is emphasized in lessons in youth classes, where the young people and their teachers can discuss them and set goals for future conduct. Thus, many forces are combined to help youth to avoid temptation and to stay morally clean.

For those who are of marriage age and older, there are guidelines as well. The Church teaches that sexual purity is the standard for all who are unmarried, and that only within the bonds of marriage may a couple be intimate. Premarital sex, petting, and anything that is contrary to the highest moral standards are forbidden. Couples are counseled to work together and to support and strengthen each other in all things in order to avoid temptations that might lead to the breaking of their sacred marriage vows. Anything that might pull spouses apart is to be avoided.

We find it comfortable and good to be on the side of time-proven Christian virtues and standards, even though the world around us might promote different standards and call us "old-fashioned." We are counseled by the Lord in modern revelation:

"Let virtue garnish thy thoughts unceasingly; then shall thy confidence wax strong in the presence of God; and the doctrine of the priesthood shall distil upon thy soul as the dews from heaven. The Holy Ghost shall be thy constant companion, and thy scepter an unchanging scepter of righteousness and truth." (D&C 121:45-46.)

Living in the world, we do recognize that temptations are strong and that some may stray from the standards established by Christ and His church. One of the principal missions of His church is to point out sin and call people to repentance. At the same time, the Church has a responsibility to reach out with the pure love of Christ to any who have transgressed, and to offer them hope, assurance, encouragement, and positive assistance that will lead them through the process of repentance. Possibly one of the greatest gifts of Christ to all mankind is that of repentance and forgiveness from God.

The whole purpose of the suffering and death of the Savior was so that He could atone for our sins. He paid the price and settled the debt in advance for whatever sin or transgression we might commit. In order to have that payment effective in our lives, we must have faith in Him, take His name upon us, promise to live His commandments, and repent of our sins and then sin no more. Through the ordinance of baptism and receiving the Holy Ghost through the laying on of hands, we enter into a contract or covenant with Him, and in return, our sins to that point are forgiven us. For sins committed after baptism, we must repent. The Lord has said, "Behold, he who has repented of his sins, the same is forgiven, and I, the Lord, remember them no more." (D&C 58:42.) The steps of repentance are:

1. Recognition of wrong. Paul called this step "godly sorrow," as opposed to being sorry because one was found out and embarrassed.

2. Resolution to change one's life to a life that is compatible with the teachings and commandments of God.

3. Confession to the Lord, to the party who has been wronged or offended, and, where the Church is concerned, to an appointed judge in Israel (defined as one's bishop or other ecclesiastic leader).

4. Restitution to those who have been offended.

5. Forsaking one's errors and replacing them with positive, Christlike habits and acts.

6. Forgiveness of any persons who have offended, and forgiveness of self.

We believe that there is hope, there is promise, there is a way back from any level of moral transgression. There is no such thing as transgression beyond repentance and forgiveness. That is what Christ and His church are all about. "Though your sins be as scarlet," He said, "they shall be as white as snow." (Isaiah 1:18.)

We Are Christians Because . . .

We Believe in Forgiveness and in Controlling Our Tongues

In the Sermon on the Mount, the Savior taught the higher law: "Ye have heard that it was said by them of old time, Thou shalt not kill; and whosoever shall kill shall be in danger of the judgment: But I say unto you, That whosoever is angry with his brother without a cause shall be in danger of the judgment." (Matthew 5:21-22.)

Together with the entire Christian world, as well as other civilizations and religions, we recognize that relationships between people must be built on mutual respect. Whenever relationships degenerate, tensions build, and anger raises its ugly head, society suffers. There is no room for anger in a family, in a neighborhood, in a city, in a nation, or between nations. Christ spoke out forcefully against anger, arguing, contentions, taking offense, or any of the many other evidences that one is losing or has lost control of his emotions. He taught that not only must we not be angry or violent in our words and actions, but also that we should agree quickly with our adversary, turn the other cheek, go the second mile, love our enemy, bless those who curse us, and pray for those who despitefully use us or persecute us.

Philosophers and religious leaders down through the ages have consistently taught that the cultured, educated, wise, and useful people of society are those who can completely control their tongues and their passions. Benjamin Franklin said, "A man in a passion rides a mad horse." I heard almost the same expression many years ago when an Argentine gaucho said, "That man who cannot tame his own anger rides a wild horse without a bridle."

Aristotle said, "Anybody can become angry . . . that is easy; but to be angry with the right person, and to the right degree, and at the right time, and for the right purpose, and in the right way, . . . that is not within everybody's power and is not easy." Another way of looking at this philosophy is to say that perhaps there are times when righteous indignation is justified, as when Christ cast the moneychangers out of the temple. He was in control all the time. He never reacted with anger when people spoke against Him, even when they took Him prisoner and crucified Him, yet when His Father's temple was desecrated, He did become righteously indignant. There are times when we too need to defend an innocent third party to or stand up for the gospel or to protect a woman's virtue or a friend's good name—but always in total control, to the right degree, at the right time, for the right purpose, and in the right way.

I like the words of Theodore M. Burton: "Whenever you get red in the face, whenever you raise your voice, whenever you get 'hot under the collar,' or angry, rebellious, or negative in spirit, then know that the Spirit [of Christ] is leaving you and the spirit of Satan is beginning to take over." (*Conference Report*, The Church of Jesus Christ of Latter-day Saints, October 1974, p. 77.) He also stated: "The longer we are members of the Church, the better we understand the Gospel, the more we will be inclined to be peacefully minded. The more diligently we follow the teachings of Christ, the slower we will be to be angry with each other and the quicker we will be to forgive each other." (*Area Conference Report*, August 1973, p. 98.)

Anger is a learned response to frustration, not the natural emotion of a mature person. Whenever we react to a situation with anger, it is not only an evil and sinful thing of the moment, but much worse is the fact that we are reinforcing a learned habit. We must turn the tendency around so that at first we can go a whole day without an angry or impatient response, then a whole week, then a month, and finally we will be so much in control that we will never get red in the face, use profanity, raise our voice, insult those around us, or do things we are afterwards sorry for. Usually the consequences of anger are much more serious than the act or deed or situation that aroused the improper passion in the first place.

Contrary to the modern thinking of some, anger is not "macho" or manly. The person who cannot control his words and actions is intemperate, untrained, immature, and uncultured. To me, mildness and gentleness, slowness to anger, and keeping control of oneself when provoked are much greater evidence that one has reached maturity and can be trusted with important matters both of the world and the kingdom of God.

Many people with quick tempers justify their reactions by saying, "Well, that is just the way I am," or "I was born that way." It may be the way they are now, it may be the way they have become, but it is certainly not the way they should be, nor is it the way the Savior wants us to be. We must change ourselves before we leave this earth life, or we will not be allowed to associate in the next life with more purified souls. We would certainly not be prepared to be in the presence of the Savior or our Heavenly Father.

The emotions of anger and of feeling offended are poisons to spirituality. They do us more harm than anything another person might do to harm us. A classic illustration is the one of the rattlesnake. If a poisonous snake bites me and flees, what should I do? Should I look for a stick or rock to punish it, or should I quickly get a tourniquet and razor blade in order to get the poison out of me? To preserve my life, I had better get the poison out of me as fast as possible!

In order to avoid letting anger poison our spirits and our personalities, we need to get the poison out by forgiving and forgetting as rapidly as we can. In addition to the damage the negative emotion can do to our spirits, there is the fact that unless we can forgive others, the Lord will not forgive us. The Savior used the parable of the unmerciful servant to illustrate this point. In this powerful story, a certain king, while making an accounting of his servants, discovered that one owed him ten thousand talents. Since the servant could not pay, the king commanded that the servant be sold along with his family so that the payment could be made. When the servant begged for mercy and said that he would get the money, the king, moved with compassion, "loosed him, and forgave him the debt." However, the servant then went out and found a fellowservant who owed him one hundred pence. He demanded payment of the debt and, when the man could not pay, had him thrown into debtors' prison. When this was reported to the king, he called the servant to him and said, "O thou wicked servant, I forgave thee all that debt, because thou desiredst me: shouldest not thou also have had compassion on thy fellowservant, even as I had pity on thee?" Angry, the king had the man "delivered . . . to his tormentor, till he should pay all that was due" to the king. The Savior concluded the parable with these words: "So likewise shall my heavenly Father do also unto you, if ye from your hearts forgive not every one his brother their trespasses." (Matthew 18:23-35.)

Our prophet, President Spencer W. Kimball, tells the following story:

> I was struggling with a community problem in a small ward . . . where two prominent men, leaders of the people, were deadlocked in a long and unrelenting feud. Some misunderstanding between them had driven them far apart with enmity. As the days, weeks, and months passed, the breach became wider. The families of each conflicting party began to take up the issue and finally nearly all the people of the ward were involved. Rumors spread and differences were aired and gossip became tongues of fire until the little community was divided by a deep gulf. I was sent to clear up the matter. After a long stake conference, lasting most of two days, I arrived at the frustrated community about six p.m., Sunday night, and immediately went into session with the principal combatants.
>
> How we struggled! How I pleaded and warned and begged and urged! Nothing seemed to be moving them. Each antagonist was so sure that he was right and justified that it was impossible to budge them.
>
> The hours were passing—it was now long after midnight, and despair seemed to enshroud the place; the atmosphere was still one of ill temper and ugliness. Stubborn resistance would not give way. Then it happened. I aimlessly opened my Doctrine and Covenants again and there before me it was. I had read it many times in past years and it had had no special meaning then. But tonight it was the very answer. It was an appeal and an imploring and a threat and seemed to be coming direct

from the Lord. I read from the seventh verse on, but the quarreling participants yielded not an inch until I came to the ninth verse. Then I saw them flinch, startled, wondering. Could that be right? The Lord was saying to us—to all of us—"Wherefore, I say unto you, that ye ought to forgive one another."

This was an obligation. They had heard it before. They had said it in repeating the Lord's Prayer. But now: ". . . for he that forgiveth not his brother his trespasses standeth condemned before the Lord. . . ." (D&C 64:7-9.)

In their hearts, they may have been saying: "Well, I might forgive if he repents and asks forgiveness, but he must make the first move." Then the full impact of the last line seemed to strike them: "For there remaineth in him the greater sin."

What? Does that mean I must forgive even if my antagonist remains cold and indifferent and mean? There is no mistaking it.

A common error is the idea that the offender must apologize and humble himself to the dust before forgiveness is required. Certainly, the one who does the injury should totally make his adjustment, but as for the offended one, he must forgive the offender regardless of the attitude of the other. Sometimes men get satisfactions from seeing the other party on his knees and grovelling in the dust, but that is not the gospel way.

Shocked, the two men sat up, listened, pondered a minute, then began to yield. This scripture added to all the others read brought them to their knees. Two a.m. and two bitter adversaries were shaking hands, smiling and forgiving and asking forgiveness. Two men were in a meaningful embrace. This hour was holy. Old grievances were forgiven and forgotten, and enemies became friends again. No reference was ever made again to the differences. The skeletons were buried, the closet of dry bones was locked and the key was thrown away, and peace was restored. (*The Teachings of Spencer W. Kimball,* Salt Lake City: Bookcraft, 1982, pp. 240-42.)

If someone insults us on purpose, that is that person's problem, and we are foolish to react and lower ourselves to the same level. If someone insults us but does not mean to do so, that is still that person's problem, and we are foolish to react. If someone did not insult us at all but we misunderstood, that is our problem, and we are foolish to react. In fact, regardless of what happens, we are foolish to react with anger or with hurt feelings or with feelings of offense. We must get the poison out. That is what the Savior wants us to do.

Since frequently the offense was not intended and the offender is not aware of what he has done to us, and since the offended one is the one with poison killing his spirit, it is logical that the offended one should make the first overtures toward peace. If we sulk, if we become inactive in the Church, if we turn bitter, we are only hurting ourselves.

In marriage, the closest and tenderest of relationships, we need to forgive very quickly and forget completely. The best solution for avoiding hurt feelings in marriage is to follow the interview system used for missionary companions. It works for anyone who works and lives with another person, such as roommates, married couples of all ages, and missionaries. No one can take constant criticism, real or implied. Feelings can be hurt and egos wounded by one person's frequently saying to the other, "Why did you do that?"—implying that whatever is questioned is not pleasing to that person. Statements such as "That was sure a dumb thing to do" can start a rift between two people that can lead to disintegration of their relationship if it is not corrected. On the other hand, in any intimate living situation there are normal differences of opinion as to whether dinner was prepared correctly, the house painted the right color, or the money spent in the "best" way. In order to avoid friction when differing points of view exist, both parties need to agree that they will avoid any real or implied criticism. No one can take daily chipping away at his or her personality and self-esteem. To achieve a meeting of the minds, both parties need to hold a regular companionship interview.

In such an interview, the senior companion—in this example, the husband—takes the initiative and says, "Honey, please share with me some ways I can be a better husband and please you more." She might tell him such things as, "Dear, it would really help me in keeping the house tidy if you would hang up your clothes and put your dirty clothes in the basket by the washer. Also, the garbage is too heavy for me, so could you help me by taking it out without my having to remind you? And then one last thing, dear, which I am sorry to mention, but when you married me you promised me at least one romantic date a week, and we have gone several weeks now just too busy to keep our courtship as alive as we both would like it." The husband must agree to do his very best to solve these little sources of irritation to his wife. She would not mention them unless they were important to her. They might not seem important to him, but that is the very essence of this approach. Since she has brought them up, he had better set up a system to remember them, calendar them, and form the desired habit pattern not to forget them.

Now it is her turn. She says, "Honey, what can I do to be a better wife?" The husband replies, "Well, dear, now that you ask, I have been wondering if you could please put the cap back on the toothpaste and keep the bathroom clear of your things so I can shave. I didn't have any sisters, and I'm not used to the way our bathroom looks. Also, my mother always cooked eggs with the yolk soft, but you cook them so the yolk is hard. You are such a perfect wife that I can't think of any other suggestions."

Some rules of this game are: no lists allowed, no written comments, and no more than three items—by memory—per interview per week. If we have prepared ourselves beforehand for constructive criticism, if we have girded our loins, so to speak, we can take almost any suggestion if it is given in a spirit of love. But if the other person just cannot change to our image of perfection, then we still have the best solution available to us: forgive, forget, and love the person just as he or she is.

Quarreling is a family sickness often seen today that needs to be completely purged from our homes. Richard L. Evans had some very pertinent thoughts on this subject:

> Life has enough problems of other kinds, for all of us, without adding quarrelling and contention. But it happens. It happens at home; it happens at work; it happens in public and private places—people quarrelling, criticizing, accusing; cutting deep wounds, saying things they shouldn't say—breaking hearts, solving nothing, hurting themselves.
>
> Quarrelling hurts especially with family and friends. It hurts when children are helplessly caught in a crossfire between two quarrelling parents—or, to use another figure, between the snipping blades of a pair of scissors. Children are so often the

victims of what adults shouldn't do. There is also the public kind of quarrelling, where the contenders seem determined to cut each other down.

Of course there are mistakes, facts to be faced—performance that isn't good enough, grievances which cannot altogether be brushed aside. But there are unkind and kinder ways of correction. And since there is no perfection in any of us, we have no right to expect it of others.

Hearts can be broken, lives blighted, homes made unhappy, and friends and families pulled apart by quarrelling and by frequent magnifying of faults. There is no peace, no pleasant place, no home, no heart that can't be hurt by quarrelling and contention. This world needs kindness, compassion, understanding. It is too cramped for two fools quarrelling. (*Thoughts for One Hundred Days*, 5 vols., Salt Lake City: Publishers Press, 1972, vol. 5, pp. 164-65.)

The scriptures have many statements concerning anger, including these:

"Cease from anger, and forsake wrath." (Psalm 38:8.)

"A wrathful man stirreth up strife: but he that is slow to anger appeaseth strife." (Proverbs 15:18.)

"He that is slow to anger is better than the mighty: and he that ruleth his spirit than he that taketh a city." (Proverbs 16:32.)

"Make no friendship with an angry man: and with a furious man thou shalt not go, lest thou learn his ways, and get a snare to thy soul." (Proverbs 22:24.)

"Let not the sun go down upon your wrath." (Ephesians 4:26.)

"Let all bitterness, and wrath, and anger, and clamour, and evil speaking be put away from you, with all malice, and be ye kind one to another, tenderhearted, forgiving one another, even as God for Christ's sake hath forgiven you." (Ephesians 4:31.)

"Fathers, provoke not your children to anger, lest they be discouraged." (Colossians 3:21.)

"He that hath the spirit of contention is not of me, but is of the devil, who is the father of contention, and he stirreth up the hearts of men to contend with anger, one with another." (3 Nephi 11:29.)

As Christians, Latter-day Saints follow the commandments of

Christ, who said: "A new commandment I give unto you, That ye love one another; as I have loved you, that ye also love one another. By this shall all men know that ye are my disciples, if ye have love one to another." (John 13:34-35.) This is our ultimate goal—to always show love to everyone by bridling our anger and keeping it under control.

We Are Christians Because . . .

We Believe in Being Self-Sufficient and in Not Coveting

As Christians, Latter-day Saints strive to obey, to the very best of their ability, the Judeo-Christian commandment, "Thou shalt not covet." (Exodus 20:17.)

Christ explained that "that which cometh out of the man, that defileth the man," included coveting. (Mark 7:20-21.) Paul stated that the love of money, a form of coveting, is the root of all evil. (1 Timothy 6:10.) Modern prophets, leaders of The Church of Jesus Christ of Latter-day Saints, preach this doctrine and add to it the wise counsel that we should each seek to be self-sufficient, prepared to meet any emergencies, quick to help others from our reserves in time of need, and generous in our offerings, which are used by the Church for helping others who are in need. If we do these things, we will not covet that which others have nor will others who are also self-sufficient have cause to covet that which we have.

To covet means to desire, to long for, to crave that which belongs to another person. Goals to acquire a comfortable home and nice furnishings, to enjoy certain comforts, to educate our children, and so forth, are not violations of the commandment so long as our priorities are in order; but the desire or impulse to take anything away from another person unlawfully is a sin, and thoughts that dwell upon others' possessions come close to the sin.

The spirit of covetousness is a kind of poison that kills the spirituality of the individual who suffers from it. We make jokes about "keeping up with the Joneses," but that too is a form of

95

coveting. The competitive spirit that causes us to want to buy a new car when our neighbor buys one borders upon unspiritual covetousness, especially if our priorities get out of line. The scripture says that we should not covet our neighbor's house, our neighbor's wife, our neighbor's servants, nor anything like unto these things.

If coveting means to take away that which another person has, then to dwell in our thoughts upon his possessions can become a kind of mental theft—not damaging to him, but certainly to us. To think about our neighbor's wife can lead to immoral thoughts, for which we will be judged. The poison of such mental concentration can destroy our sense of balance between right and wrong and lead to serious sins. Probably the most famous story demonstrating this trend was the downfall of the great King David. He was a good and righteous person until he coveted the beautiful wife of another man, the soldier Uriah. The poison warped David's mind to such a degree that he actually conspired to set up a scheme to put Uriah in the front lines of battle where he would be killed. A military leader has to make some difficult decisions, but David's act of coldly exposing a soldier to certain death, not for military advantage but so that he, David, could have his widow, was considered by the Lord as murder.

Probably no one is possessed of the spirit of covetousness when he starts out just thinking about his neighbor's lovely home or fine car or prosperous business. However, Satan has a way of taking such idle thoughts and turning them into envy, and finally downgrading them into covetousness. Sometimes people tend to justify their thoughts about others' possessions as mere ambition or goal setting. And it is true that good goals and a reasonable desire to improve our economic position plus providing well for our loved ones is a worthy stimulus to hard work, prudent savings, and wise investments, but beware lest things get out of control. The moment a person starts to think that another person does not deserve that which he has accumulated, he is on the dangerous edge of coveting, and if he continues to desire what his neighbor has, he has slipped over the brink and has opened himself to the full spirit of covetousness, which is controlled by Satan.

A higher interpretation of this commandment is found in the

book of revelations known as the Doctrine and Commandments, where the Lord says to Martin Harris, "Thou shalt not covet thine own property." (D&C 20:26.) In addition to not coveting what is rightfully someone else's, the Lord is saying that we should be generous with our own property. Martin Harris was commanded to give freely of his assets so that the Book of Mormon could be printed and sent forth into the world. Martin understood, and he provided the necessary funds. Each of us should come to an understanding that the Lord expects us not to covet that which we have earned or inherited, but that we should be generous in giving to the poor, the needy, our families and loved ones, and the Church as well as its institutions.

In the Book of Mormon, King Benjamin outlined a welfare plan for his people, a plan that is applicable to us as well:

"Succor those that stand in need of your succor; . . . administer of your substance unto him that standeth in need; and . . . not suffer that the beggar putteth up his petition to you in vain, [nor] turn him out to perish.

"Perhaps thou shalt say: The man has brought upon himself this misery; therefore I will stay my hand, and will not give unto him of my food, nor impart unto him of my substance that he may not suffer, for his punishments are just—

"But I say unto you, O man, whosoever doeth this the same hath great cause to repent; and except he repenteth of that which he hath done he perisheth forever, and hath no interest in the kingdom of God.

"For behold, are we not all beggars? Do we not all depend upon the same Being, even God, for all the substance which we have, for both food and raiment, and for gold, and for silver, and for all the riches which we have of every kind?" (Mosiah 4:16-19. See also Mosiah 18:27-29.)

An extension of the parable of the prodigal son (see Luke 15:11-32) illustrates well an additional dimension to the principle of generosity. You remember that the younger son asked his father for his inheritance, even before the father was close to dying. What an ungrateful son, to insinuate to his father that he would prefer the father to die soon by saying to him, "Give me the portion of goods that falleth to me." The son then went off with his money to a far country, and there he "wasted his substance with riotous living." We can imagine the tragedy that unfolded. The young man's life went from bad to worse—from riches to abject poverty, from high social position among temporary friends to the feeding of swine, and from the feeding of the pigs to the eating of the garbage he was feeding them. Finally, after sinking so low, the young man came to his senses, realized his errors as well as his sins, and turned to repentance. He decided to return home to offer himself to his father as a servant. He well knew he could ask no more.

I can imagine the sorrowing father watching the horizon for days and even months on end, praying for his errant son to come home. And then it happened. The father, through dimmed vision, thought he saw a familiar figure far in the distance. As the figure drew nearer, he could see that it was his son coming home. The father, with tears of emotion, ran toward the son and hugged him, kissed him tenderly, and heard the contrite confession, "Father, I have sinned against heaven, and in thy sight, and am no more worthy to be called thy son."

The father would not hear of this. He called his servants to bring the best robe to dress his son, a ring for his finger, and shoes for his feet. He also ordered the fatted calf, saying, "Let us eat, and be merry: for this my son was dead, and is alive again; he was lost, and is found."

The man's older son, who had apparently been working in the fields until late, came home and noticed all the festivities, which had by this time turned into a full-fledged party with music and dancing. A servant told him that his brother had returned home and that this was what his father had ordered. The older son became so upset that he refused to go inside. When his father came out to him, the son said, "Lo, these many years do I serve thee, neither transgressed I at any time thy commandment: and yet thou never gavest me a kid, that I might make merry with my friends." The father, probably recognizing the implied injustice of the past but not knowing quite what to do, said, "Son, thou art ever with me, and all that I have is thine. It was meet that we should make merry, and be glad: for this thy brother was dead, and is alive again; and was lost, and is found."

In my mind I can see the older brother struggle with mixed

emotions. Of course he loved his dear father and was happy to see the joy in his father's face. But he was also disturbed by the apparent lack of fairness and probably jealous of so much attention being given to his younger brother. I am sure he wondered why his father had not given him similar recognition and signs of love.

In my fictitious ending to this story, at this point the younger brother comes out and makes a gesture of reconciliation, maybe even offers to be a servant to his brother. Gone is the old rivalry on his part. He is now more mature, more humble, more contrite, especially more spiritual. I can see him saying something to indicate that he, the younger, loves and respects his older brother and appreciates his staying home to take care of their father. I can imagine something happening that tugs at the heartstrings of the offended older brother to the point where he is suddenly filled with love toward his father and forgiveness toward his errant brother. He turns to his father and says, "Father, divide my inheritance with my brother. I too rejoice that he is back. There is more than enough for all of us."

Now in my scenario I can see the double joy and excitement of the father. He shouts to the servants, "Bring my very best robes and rings and the new boots I had made for myself. Put them on my eldest son, and then go kill another fatted calf, and call all the friends of this my eldest son, that they too may come for a grand party. He who might have been lost to covetousness and selfishness is found—he has found himself in generosity. Yea, we who were lost to each other have now found each other. Let us join in celebrating our newfound family unity, our brotherhood."

One of the opposites of covetousness is generosity. There is a great need in the world today for more generosity. We can be more generous at home in the family circle. We can be more generous with our relatives. We can be more generous with our neighbors and our fellow employees. (Remember, Scrooge was coveting his own assets until the spirits of Christmas frightened him and turned him into a generous person.) We can be more generous with all with whom we come into contact.

The tendency to want more things for ourselves is a kind of egotism and selfishness. It is apparently a sign of the last days, for Paul warned, "In the last days perilous times shall come. For men shall be lovers of their own selves, covetous." (2 Timothy 3:1-2.) There is no doubt that our civilization is in a race to acquire more and more personal wealth and comforts.

The words of the Savior on this subject are powerful, even scathing: "Wo unto you poor men, whose hearts are not broken, whose spirits are not contrite, and whose bellies are not satisfied, and whose hands are not stayed from laying hold upon other men's goods, whose eyes are full of greediness, and who will not labor with your own hands!" (D&C 56:17.) Our present social programs tend to cause the beneficiaries of welfare payments to lose interest in work, labor, sacrifice, and savings. One who receives something for nothing tends to become less contrite and more demanding, and he wants the things that others have without paying for them or working for them.

One of our modern temptations is to buy now and pay later. "Unwarrantable installment buying is a pit into which those who covet fall," said Elder John H. Vandenberg in a general conference talk. (*Conference Report,* October 1966, p. 68.) The problem is that when we buy on credit, we incur interest payments, which increase the cost of the item to us, sometimes to the point where we pay two or three times the original price of the item.

In the early days of the Church, the Lord gave the Latter-day Saints an economic plan for a high level of spiritual living. This plan, called the United Order, became doomed to failure because some who practiced it did not have the dedication and mature understanding needed to overcome the spirit of covetousness. The Lord declared: "The covenants being broken through transgression, by covetousness and feigned words—therefore you are dissolved as a united order." (D&C 104:52-53.)

When we see someone else prosper, we should not judge him nor worry about his righteousness. If his example is good, we might learn from it. If his example is not in accord with the commandments, we should not follow it. In Psalms, we read: "Rest in the Lord, and wait patiently for him: fret not thyself because of him who prospereth in his way." (Psalms 37:7.)

Laziness is often related to coveting. In Proverbs we read, "The desire of the slothful killeth him; for his hands refuse to labour. He coveteth greedily all the day long: but the righteous giveth and spareth not." (Proverbs 21:25-26.) Generosity is the opposite of covetousness. Generosity builds up treasures in heaven where they are of eternal value to us, while covetousness only leads to treasures on earth, where moth and rust corrupt and where thieves break through and steal. Jesus tells us, "Take heed, and beware of covetousness: for a man's life consisteth not in the abundance of the things which he possesseth." (Luke 12:15.)

So serious is the sin of coveting that Paul even advised against those who do so. In order to lift ourselves to higher spiritual levels, we must associate with those who are pure in heart, not be drawn down by persons who are not motivated by spiritual things. Paul said to the Corinthians, "I wrote to you in an epistle not to company with . . . the covetous." (1 Corinthians 5:9-10.) In Colossians Paul gives us an additional dimension or definition of covetousness. He says it is idolatry. (Colossians 3:5.) Some people worship possessions. They become obsessed with temporal goals and ambitions to the exclusion of family, friends, church, community, business, and all else. But those who covet material things will eventually pay the price; the time of reckoning will come.

Our prophets have told us that in order to avoid coveting others' goods, we should be independent and self-reliant. We should be prepared for emergencies with enough food and clothing on hand to take care of our own families should normal trade, transportation, and supplies ever be interrupted. We should also prepare for our own needs should the principal provider ever become incapacitated due to health problems, an accident, or loss of job. This attitude of being prepared blesses us two ways: it helps us meet emergencies and it helps us avoid covetousness. An even greater extension of this principle is to be prepared not only to meet our own needs, but to help meet the needs of others also.

Jesus came to give us a higher law. How blessed are those who can build their lives on His teachings and strive for the blessings that are not of this world, who seek first His kingdom and His righteousness. They will not covet anything temporal, but will lay claim to the great reward that He has promised: "All these things shall be added unto you!"

We Are Christians Because . . .

We Believe in and Attempt to Follow All of Christ's Ideals for Living

The thirteenth Article of Faith of The Church of Jesus Christ of Latter-day Saints declares: "We believe in being honest, true, chaste, benevolent, virtuous, and in doing good to all men. . . . If there is anything virtuous, lovely, or of good report or praiseworthy, we seek after these things."

We accept and strive to live all the Christlike virtues exemplified in the Beatitudes, the Sermon on the Mount, and all of Christ's teachings. We believe that we should serve Him with all our heart, might, mind, and strength; that we should be examples of faith, charity, love, virtue, knowledge, temperance, patience, brotherly kindness, godliness, humility, and diligence, always having an eye single to the glory of God.

We believe that before He came to earth to be born of Mary, Christ was in heaven at the right hand of God the Father. We also believe that Christ was the authorized spokesman for the Godhead and was the agent acting under the direction of the Father in the creation of the earth. We believe that the Father sent Christ, as Jehovah, to appear and speak to ancient prophets. Therefore, it was Christ, as Jehovah, who appeared before Moses in the burning bush and again on the mountain, and it was He who, with His finger, engraved the Ten Commandments upon the tablets of stone.

We believe that He came to earth in the meridian of time, was born of Mary, and was baptized at the beginning of His ministry by John the Baptist. We believe that He taught His gospel to His disciples and to others as they gathered on the hillside, by the road, and in the towns and villages. We believe that He established His church, based on His gospel, while He was on earth, and that that same church continued to grow and flourish in the Mediterranean world after His crucifixion and resurrection, through the ministry of Peter, Paul, and other prophets and apostles. We believe that an apostasy from the pristine church that He established took place in the centuries after the deaths of the apostles, and that this was followed by a long period of darkness, or cessation of light and knowledge from the Father. We believe that that same church was restored to the earth in the early nineteenth century through the instrumentality of Joseph Smith, and that today, as The Church of Jesus Christ of Latter-day Saints, it is continuing to grow and to draw unto it persons of many nationalities and persuasions, all of whom accept its divine teachings.

Among the teachings of Jesus Christ that He taught during His earthly ministry and that are still in force among His followers today are those embodied in the Sermon on the Mount. It is the greatest collection of Christian virtues ever compiled in one place, the model of that which Christ exemplifies as well as that which we should try to emulate. We believe that in these teachings, Jesus established a higher law to supersede the law of Moses. The earlier commandments, which are still in force as God's law, have a "thou shalt not" approach, for Israel was not prepared for the higher law. In contrast, the Sermon on the Mount is full of love and tenderness. It is our guide toward the higher Christian ethic. Among the many teachings embodied in it are the following, all of which we subscribe to and strive to keep in our lives as His disciples today:

The Beatitudes

"Blessed are the poor in spirit, for theirs is the kingdom of heaven.

"Blessed are they that mourn: for they shall be comforted.

"Blessed are the meek: for they shall inherit the earth.

"Blessed are they which do hunger and thirst after righteousness, for they shall be filled.

"Blessed are the merciful: for they shall obtain mercy.

"Blessed are the pure in heart: for they shall see God.

"Blessed are the peacemakers: for they shall be called the children of God.

"Blessed are they which are persecuted for righteousness' sake: for theirs is the kingdom of heaven." (Matthew 5:2-10.)

The Missionary Commandments

"Ye are the salt of the earth." (Matthew 5:13.) We are to go forth doing good among men and lifting all with whom we come in contact. Even one person can do so much good that he or she can actually change the flavor of the environment in which he or she lives and works.

"Ye are the light of the world. . . . Let your light so shine before men that they may see your good works, and glorify your Father which is in heaven." (Matthew 5:14, 16.) We should each live a model life as an example to others.

Five Higher Laws

1. "Ye have heard that it was said by them of old time, Thou shalt not kill; and whosoever shall kill shall be in danger of judgment. But I say unto you that whosoever is angry with his brother without a cause shall be in danger of the judgment: . . . and whosoever shall say, Thou fool, shall be in danger of hell fire. . . . Agree with thine adversary quickly." (Matthew 5:21-25.)

2. "Ye have heard that it was said by them of old time, Thou shalt not commit adultery: But I say unto you, That whosoever looketh on a woman to lust after her hath committed adultery with her already in his heart." (Matthew 5:27-28.)

3. "Ye have heard that it hath been said by them of old time, Thou shalt not forswear thyself, but shall perform unto the Lord thine oaths: But I say unto you, *Swear not at all*; neither by heaven; for it is God's throne; nor by the earth; for it is his footstool. . . . But let your communication be, Yea, yea; Nay, nay: for whatsoever is more than these cometh of evil." (Matthew 5:33-37. Italics added.) If we watch our own tongues, we will not get angry with ourselves and we will not knowingly offend others.

4. "Ye have heard that it hath been said, An eye for an eye, and a tooth for a tooth: But I say unto you, That ye resist not evil:

but whosoever shall smite thee on thy right cheek, turn to him the other also. And if any man will sue thee at the law, and take away thy coat, let him have thy cloke also. And whosoever shall compel thee to go a mile, go with him twain. Give to him that asketh thee, and from him that would borrow of thee turn not away." (Matthew 5:38-42.) This higher law of retribution is based on Christ's message of love and consideration for our fellowman.

5. "Ye have heard that it hath been said, Thou shalt love thy neighbor, and hate thine enemy. But I say unto you, Love your enemies, bless them that curse you, do good to them that hate you, and pray for them which despitefully use you, and persecute you; that ye may be the children of your Father which is in heaven: . . . For if ye love them which love you, what reward have ye? do not even the publicans the same?" (Matthew 5:43-46.) We must love *all* persons, regardless of how they act toward us or how they may feel about us. We must not just love those who love us.

At this point in His Sermon on the Mount, the Savior interjected that jewel of a commandment, all-inclusive and overwhelming in implications and responsibilities for us, that declares our highest goal: "Be ye therefore perfect, even as your Father which is in heaven is perfect." (Matthew 5:48.) This is especially important to us, because we know that God never gives a commandment unless he provides a way for us to ultimately live that commandment.

Three Rules of Sincerity versus Hypocrisy

1. "Take heed that ye do not your alms before men, to be seen of them: otherwise ye have no reward of your Father which is in heaven. . . . But when thou doest alms, let not thy left hand know what thy right hand doeth: that thine alms may be in secret: and thy Father which seeth in secret himself shall reward thee openly." (Matthew 6:1-4.) If we are generous only in order to be seen of others, we will get our reward only from others and not from our Heavenly Father.

2. "And when thou prayest, thou shalt not be as the hypocrites are: for they love to pray standing in the synagogues and in the corners of the streets, that they may be seen of men. Verily I

say unto you, They have their reward. But thou, when thou prayest, . . . pray unto thy Father . . . in secret; and thy Father which seeth in secret shall reward thee openly. But when ye pray, use not vain repetitions, as the heathen do: for they think that they shall be heard for their much speaking. Be not ye therefore like unto them: for your Father knoweth what things ye have need of, before ye ask him." (Matthew 6:5-8.) The Savior then gives the prayer known as the "Lord's Prayer."

3. "Moreover when ye fast, be not, as the hypocrites, of a sad countenance: for they disfigure their faces, that they may appear unto men to fast. Verily I say unto you, They have their reward. But thou, when thou fastest, . . . fast . . . unto thy Father which is in secret: and thy Father, which seeth in secret, shall reward thee openly." (Matthew 6:16-18.)

Guidelines on Money and Material Possessions

1. "Lay not up for yourselves treasures upon earth, where moth and rust doth corrupt, and where thieves break through and steal: But lay up for yourselves treasures in heaven, . . . for where your treasure is, there will your heart be also." (Matthew 6:19-21.)

2. "No man can serve two masters: for either he will hate the one and love the other; or else he will hold to the one, and despise the other. Ye cannot serve God and mammon." (Matthew 6:24.)

3. "Seek ye first the kingdom of God, and his righteousness; and all these things shall be added unto you." (Matthew 6:33.) If we follow His commandments and serve our fellowman and Him, we will be blessed with those blessings that we stand in need of.

Individual Gems of Spiritual Behavior

1. "Judge not, that ye be not judged. . . . And why beholdest thou the mote that is in thy brother's eye, but considerest not the beam that is in thine own eye?" (Matthew 7:1, 3.)

2. "Give not that which is holy unto the dogs, neither cast ye your pearls before swine." (Matthew 7:6.)

3. "Ask, and it shall be given you; seek, and ye shall find; knock, and it shall be opened unto you: for everyone that asketh receiveth; and he that seeketh findeth; and to him that knocketh

it shall be opened." (Matthew 7:7-8.)

4. "All things whatsoever ye would that men should do to you, do ye even so to them: for this is the law and the prophets." (Matthew 7:12.) Note that this beautiful verse has come to be known as the "golden rule."

5. "Enter ye in at the strait [narrow] gate: for wide is the gate, and broad is the way, that leadeth to destruction. . . . Strait is the gate, and narrow is the way, which leadeth unto life." (Matthew 7:13-14.)

6. "Beware of false prophets, which come to you in sheep's clothing, but inwardly they are ravening wolves. Ye shall know them by their fruits. . . . Every good tree bringeth forth good fruit; but a corrupt tree bringeth forth evil fruit." (Matthew 7:15, 17.)

7. "Not every one that saith unto me, Lord, Lord, shall enter into the kingdom of heaven; but he that doeth the will of my Father which is in heaven." (Matthew 7:21.)

8. "Whosoever heareth these sayings of mine, and doeth them, I will liken him unto a wise man, which built his house upon a rock: and the rain descended, and the floods came, and the winds blew, and beat upon that house; and it fell not: for it was founded upon a rock." (Matthew 7:24-25.)

Additional Godly Attributes

In 1829, the Prophet Joseph Smith received a revelation from the Lord in which additional godly attributes were enumerated:

"Therefore, O ye that embark in the service of God, see that ye serve him with all your heart, might, mind and strength, that ye may stand blameless before God at the last day. . . .

"And faith, hope, charity and love, with an eye single to the glory of God, qualify him for the work.

"Remember faith, virtue, knowledge, temperance, patience, brotherly kindness, godliness, charity, humility, diligence." (D&C 4:2, 5-6.)

Becoming a Disciple of Christ

With so many Christ-like virtues, one might wonder how to seek after these beautiful qualities of personality and character.

We Are Christians Because . . .

The most simple and direct approach for the sincere disciple of Christ is found in these three challenges:

1. Fill your mind with thoughts of the Savior. Fill your mind with the kind of noble, good, uplifting thoughts that He would want us all to have. To do this, read about His life and teachings in the four Gospels—Matthew, Mark, Luke, and John—in the New Testament, and in Third Nephi in the Book of Mormon. Read everything else you can find about the life and teachings of the Son of God. Make these things part of your personal, much-used library. In addition, you might mark pertinent chapters and passages from Sunday School lesson manuals and other sources on His life and ministry. Come to know the Shepherd, and your thoughts will turn to Him more and more frequently. As a man thinketh, so he will become. Daily scripture study and reading the best books about the Redeemer will mold character in a Christ-like way.

2. Fill your heart with love of the Savior. Develop toward your neighbor the kind of love that He exemplified. Christ-like love for others is the spirit of charity. If we love him, we will keep His commandments. Peter was told that if he loved the Savior, he should demonstrate his love by "feeding His sheep." As we develop in this area, Christ-like love and all the other attributes He exemplified will mature and grow within us.

3. Fill your life with service to Christ and to those about you. We must each become a Good Samaritan rather than the "priest" or the "Levite." We should serve even the least of our brothers and sisters as though we were serving the Savior himself. We will never know Him unless we have served Him. We will never develop His characteristics and personality traits unless He is in our every act, our every thought.

Through following these paths, bad men become good, and good men become better; the sinner becomes a saint; people fulfill their intended destiny; the gospel rolls forward like a growing snowball to fill the whole earth—all because Jesus Christ, the Son of the living God, came to earth and showed us the way, His way. We testify that He lives, that He is on the right hand of God, that He is resurrected, glorified, and exalted, and that He stands at the head of His church, which bears His name.

Index